Sunderland Museum
The People's Palace in the Park

by L. Jessop & N.T. Sinclair

Sunderland Museum & Art Gallery (Tyne & Wear Museums), Borough Road, Sunderland, Tyne & Wear SR1 1PP.

ISBN 0 905974 65 4

Front Cover: A view of the Winter Gardens from Mowbray Park at the turn of the century.

Cover designed by Alex Handy of Rufus Abajas.

FOREWORD

When Sunderland Corporation took over the collections of the Sunderland Antiquarian and Natural History Society, it acquired the first local authority run museum in the country outside London. The Corporation's aim in 1846 was to operate a Museum for "the instruction and amusement of the inhabitants of the Borough".

This book, which has been written by Les Jessop, the Keeper of Biology for Tyne & Wear Museums, and Neil Sinclair, Senior Curator of Sunderland Museums, outlines the history of the Museum from its origins in one room in the Subscription Library on High Street West to the new building on the edge of Mowbray Park in 1879 and the major extension of 1964. It marks the 150th Anniversary of Sunderland Museum and Art Gallery, and the start of another major phase of development, in the former library area.

The history of Sunderland Museum has not been one of continuous developments; there have been periods of slow progress, partly reflecting economic depression in the 1920s and 1930s. There have also been periods of remarkable progress. The book outlines the main events in the Museum's development, as well as recording curators and other personalities since 1846. The photographs, from the Museum's collection, show the way things were and how they have changed.

Unlike several other museums in the region, Sunderland Museum has had few major benefactors. The building was financed by the Corporation and only a handful of wealthy industrial and business families have bequeathed major collections. In many ways this has been one of the Museum's strengths as its development has depended on the support of the people of Wearside, expressed through the Council.

The last quarter of a century has been a time of major change for Sunderland. The town has become a city, and traditional industries, notably shipbuilding and coalmining, have disappeared, while new industries such as the manufacture of cars have been introduced. The city centre has changed dramatically and has lost familiar landmarks including the old Town Hall. Meanwhile the Museum has remained intact during this period of change and is still one of the best-loved buildings in Sunderland. Internally, there have been award-winning new displays, and access developments, which have transformed the Museum and will help to take it forward into the next 150 years.

Councillor Don Price
Chairman, Tyne and Wear Joint Museums Committee

Councillor Ralph Baxter
Vice-Chairman, Tyne and Wear Joint Museums Committee

Dr. David Fleming
Director, Tyne and Wear Museums

ACKNOWLEDGEMENTS

We would like to thank Tom Shaw and Jim Wilson for reading through drafts: their reminiscences filled several gaps in the story of the Museum. Carol Roberton of *Sunderland Echo* also very kindly read through the book, and offered her opinion as a professional writer and long-term friend of the Museum. Alan Brett of *Black Cat Publications* provided much assistance in formulating the layout of the book.

We should like to thank Marjorie Elwen, Geoffrey Milburn and the Local Studies section of the City Library for their help in the book's production.

Several members of Tyne & Wear Museums also helped: Social Historian Martin Routledge searched out many photographs and commented on the text, and Juliet Horsley and Susan Newell of the Art department contributed much on the history of the collections of fine and applied art.

The photograph of the logs in the Art Gallery and of L.S. Lowry by courtesy of the Sunderland Echo and of the guided walk over the Victoria Viaduct by Ian S. Carr. The other photographs are from Tyne and Wear Museums' collections.

INTRODUCTION

1996 sees the 150th anniversary of the corporation-run museum in Sunderland, the oldest publicly-funded museum in the country outside of London. We are taking the opportunity of the sesquicentennial to look back at the history of the Museum and at what has been achieved.

There had been a small private museum in the town since the turn of the 19th Century, but when the town council took charge of it in 1846 money became available (through the rates) to improve and expand it considerably. Originally housed in a single small room, by 1879 the contents of museum had expanded enormously and an impressive new building was built to house it. That building, still standing today, has seen some changes over the years, especially the destruction of the Winter Gardens in the 1940s and a major development scheme in the 1960s that involved re-modelling the interior and the addition of an extension that made Sunderland Museum one of the largest municipal museums in the country.

Founded with the aim of "diffusing taste and knowledge amongst our fellow townsmen" (which of course has always included women and children), since from the middle of the 19th century the museum has always been accessible to all of the people of Sunderland and not just restricted to 'the elite'. One curator could boast that during the time he had been in charge (1905-1939) there had been over 4,500,000 visitors, and in 1995 alone 173,455 people passed through the doors. With that in mind, we also take a look at the displays and exhibitions, to see what has kept the visitors coming over the years.

The exterior of the Museum was illuminated in 1935 for Jubilee celebrations on the 25th anniversary of the accession of George V and Queen Mary to the throne.

ONE

THE ORIGINS OF SUNDERLAND MUSEUM

Why have a Museum?

It seems to be part of human nature to gather together beautiful or unusual things, objects of scientific or artistic interest, or things that arouse our curiosity. For some people, the hobby of collecting can become an important part of their lives, or an obsession, and they often leave behind large and important collections.

During the 1700s and 1800s it became fashionable among the wealthier classes to make collections of antiquities (most usually, objects from ancient Greece and Rome), of paintings and of natural history objects (especially, shells and butterflies). A number of academic societies also sprang up at that time, and many of them wanted to have a museum for the use of their members. Many of the early privately assembled collections passed eventually to societies or, in some cases, to local authorities. Some of the largest became part of the great national museums like the British Museum in London.

When a museum is in private hands it is limited by the interest of the collector and by how much money is available to build the collection. Some people might only collect coins, others porcelain or paintings or butterflies. Because public museums acquire material from a range of donors, they often have collections of all these things, and Sunderland is no exception. Once the collection becomes public property and its upkeep is financed out of public funds its continued existence must be justified: governments and local councils will not usually spend money without a good reason!

The Museum building between 1884 and 1900. The cab rank was then on Holmeside, but a shelter was later built on Borough Road at the front of the Museum.

An old, but useful, definition of the purpose of a museum is that it is 'a place for the education and amusement of the public'. A similar phrase was used by Sunderland Council in 1846, when they planned a museum "for the instruction and amusement of the inhabitants of the borough". In this context, *education* does not mean sitting in a schoolroom or being taught by a teacher, it means having displays, of suitably labelled objects, that people can use if they want to find out more about the world. Also, to *amuse* visitors to a museum you don't have to tell jokes or have computer games (although some museums do have these things), but you should have displays that cause people to wonder at and *muse over*.

Education has to be balanced against amusement. If you only set out to educate, the museum can be dry, dusty and lacking in interest. If you try too hard to amuse, you reduce the displays to the level of a theme park or amusement arcade. The best museums educate and amuse at the same time.

Incidentally, although most of us think of a museum as being a building containing objects to be looked at, the word *museum* can be used to refer to the collection of objects housed in the building. So, when we speak of the museum moving from Fawcett Street to Borough Road, it is the collection, not the building that moves.

The origins of Sunderland Museum

In the late 1700s, academic societies sprang up in many towns and cities. Mostly aimed at attracting the wealthier citizens of the town as members, they often used 'Literary', 'Philosophical' or 'Antiquarian' in their title. Although many of them started off with high ideals, most had a short life and in a few years they often degenerated into gentlemen's social clubs and newspaper reading rooms - a notable exception being the Newcastle Literary and Philosophical Society, which began in 1793 and is still going strong. A Subscription Library, founded in Sunderland in 1794, and the Subscription Museum (founded March 13th, 1810) were the local examples of this movement

The Subscription Museum and Library shared a building on High Street West (between Nile Street and Norfolk Street) acquired by the Subscription Library in 1801. The museum was supported through gifts from its members and by their subscriptions. There were 36 subscribers in 1810, but by 1819 this number had fallen to five. In 1821 it was decided to close the venture, and the collection was handed over to the Subscription Library.

A catalogue of the Sunderland Subscription Museum was published in 1825, and shows that the collections mainly comprised items of natural history interest:

Mammals: There were 34 specimens, including part of the skin of the single-horned rhinoceros; skull and horns of the urus (or wild ox); backbone of an ass; skin of a zebra; pieces of whale skin.

Birds: 72 specimens, mainly British species, but including a humming-bird in its nest and the head and neck of a bird of paradise.

Amphibia and Reptiles: 17 specimens, including an alligator, several snakes and tortoise shells.

Fishes: 12 specimens

Insects and other invertebrates: Several insects in two cases, a spider, a scorpion and four crabs; a roundworm and a leach; a sea mouse and sea cucumber; six corals.

Sea shells were very popular collectors items in those days, and there was probably a large number of them in the museum, but they are not listed individually in the catalogue.

Plants: Two volumes of dried plants; nine specimens of bark cloth from Tahiti (in all probability brought back from one of Captain Cook's voyages!); sixteen specimens of wood from different trees; wood from the submerged forest at Seaton Carew; a fungus and a lichen.

Minerals and Fossils:This was the greatest part of the museum, with 427 specimens. One of the fossils is particularly interesting, as it still survives in the museum today. It is number 171 "*Brown Dolomite, or Magnesian Limestone,* with the petrifaction of a fish; also counterpart of ditto. - *From Pallion Quarry, near Sunderland*, presented by J. Goodchild". This is a fossil fish of a rare species, now known as *Platysomus striatus*.

Antiquities and Curiosities: After the natural history collections, the antiquities and 'curiosities' were listed. These included 41 very miscellaneous items such as Colonel Lilburne's boots (which are still on display today!); Chinese coins; arrows, spears etc. from different parts of the world; model of a canoe; a chinaman's pigtail, and an axe 'used by the Druids in their sacrifices'. Also of interest is a pair of garters worn by the Queen of Tahiti which, like the bark cloth, was probably brought back from one of Captain Cook's voyages.

From High Street to Fawcett Street, via Villiers Street

The Subscription Library did not take care of the museum for long, and it passed into the hands of the Sunderland Natural History and Antiquarian Society (SNH&AS), probably shortly after this latter society was founded on November 17th, 1836.

Most of the specimens in the museum at that time were Natural History objects. They would be more of interest to the SNH&AS than to the bookish subscribers to the Library. The library rooms possibly also became cramped as more books were acquired - a very common complaint in libraries through the ages - and the members wanted to get rid of the museum to create more space.

It appears that the SNH&AS didn't have their own premises in the early days, and the museum was housed in the rooms of the Sunderland Literary & Philosophical Society in Villiers Street.

The collections continued to expand: the introduction to the first annual report of the SNH&AS in 1837 noted that the museum contained 950 specimens of the 'several departments' of mineralogy and geology, zoology, conchology and antiquities.

The first home of the Subscription Museum and Subscription Library on High Street West, between Norfolk Street and Nile Street. There is no longer a building on the site.

By the time of the second report of the SNH&AS in 1843, the society had moved from Villiers Street to a much grander building, The Athenaeum (in Fawcett Street), which opened in 1840. Although the museum had not yet moved, the report claimed that they hoped "to be able to remove the cases into it in the course of a few weeks".

After only three years in the Athenaeum, the ownership of the museum again changed hands. Following the Museums Act of 1845, local councils were enabled to run museums financed from the rates, and the SNH&AS was very eager to transfer the running of its museum to the Corporation

The Athenaeum. The sign advertising the Corporation Free Library dates the photograph as probably being before 1879.

Fawcett Street looking towards Mowbray Park, before the Museum was built. The building on the left is the Athenaeum, home of the Museum from the 1840s until 1879. At that time Fawcett Street was a mainly residential area, Binns' stores were later built on both sides of the street.

TWO

CORPORATION TAKEOVER AND A NEW BUILDING

The Museums Act, 1845

The Museums Act of 1845 allowed corporations of towns with a population greater than 10,000 to raise a halfpenny on the rates in order to establish and run a museum, and to charge up to one penny entrance fee.

In 1850, the Museums Act was superseded by the Public Libraries and Museums Act. In future, a two-thirds majority of voting ratepayers had to agree to adopting the act before a museum could be run by the corporation, but by that time there was already a Public Museum in Sunderland. The 1850 act also removed the ability to charge the 1d admission fee.

Talks between Sunderland Corporation and SNH&AS about the transfer of the museum began in June 1845. On 9 July 1845 a general meeting of SNH&AS agreed to hand over the museum to the Corporation. At the same time Robert Vint presented his private collection of minerals, worth £100.

A committee was appointed in May 1846, and at a meeting of the town council on May 20th, it was resolved that "the council establish a museum of art and science for the instruction and amusement of the inhabitants of the borough under the provisions of 899 Vict cap 43". An honorary curator was appointed in September 1846 and a halfpenny was levied on the rates from November 9th. The date of foundation of Sunderland's local authority-run museum is usually taken as November 9th 1846.

Only one other town council was quick to take advantage of the new Act. The town council of Colchester, Essex, also agreed in May 1846 to provide space in the Town Hall "or some other place, for the deposit of articles of antiquity or curiosity intended for a museum to be erected in this town", but their museum was not opened to the public until September 27th, 1860.

The collection was not removed from the Athenaeum building at the time of the takeover, and the Corporation was to be charged £10 a year rent for the rooms it occupied. On October 27th 1846 it was decided to transfer the whole museum into a single room in the Athenaeum, known as the Commission Room.

Sunderland Corporation was solely responsible for running the Museum from 1846 until the local government reforms of the 1970s, when the Tyne and Wear County Council Museums Service was formed as a department of the county council. Although Tyne and Wear County Council was abolished in 1986, it was decided to keep the Museums Service as a body jointly run by committee drawn from the five district councils.

From Fawcett Street to Borough Road

The collections continued to grow at the Athenaeum, and in 1858 the Corporation also opened a Public Library in the same building. It was soon realised that the Athenaeum was too small for the long-term future of the Museum, and a new building was needed.

In July 1855, it was proposed to build a 'Crystal Palace' in Mowbray Park, and the corporation wanted to set rooms aside in it for the Museum. Unfortunately these plans came to nothing, but they may have influenced the final decision to build a Winter Gardens plus Museum and Library on a single site.

By the 1870s, it was realised that a new, purpose-built building was needed to hold the Museum and Library. The new proposal was to build in Mowbray Park - actually, strictly speaking in *Extension Park*, which comprises that part of Mowbray Park to the north of the railway line - council offices as well as Library, School of Art, Museum and Winter Gardens.

FLINTOFF'S UNVEILING OF JOHN CANDLISH MONT. SLAND.

Mowbray Park from Building Hill, before the Museum was built. The lower part, Extension Park, has already been laid out as a public park.

The Museum in 1879. The photograph can be dated because of work in progress on the railway, which opened in the same year. Notice the horses and cabs waiting in a rank on Burdon Road. The wall at the side of the building was soon removed, and the railings at the front moved back.

In 1855 Edward Backhouse proposed building a 'Crystal Palace' at the southern end of Mowbray Park, and the scheme incorporated a museum. Although nothing came directly of the 'Crystal Palace' plans, the Museum and Winter Gardens built in 1879 were possibly inspired by it.

Objections were raised to erecting buildings on the Park, which some people wanted to keep as a green space. The case was referred in December 1875 to the Chancery Division of the High Court.

The court's ruling was that the Park could only be used for "recreation ground for the people of Sunderland, and for purposes connected there with. None of the buildings contemplated by the Corporation were permissible except the museum and conservatory. These latter could be erected on any suitable spot within the discretion of the defendants [the Corporation]. The Corporation were able to do that, but were not able to transport their municipal offices to the park from some other portion of the town of Sunderland. An injunction would therefore be granted restraining the Corporation from using any portion of the park for any erection or building other than a museum or conservatory."

On appeal in March 1876, the Appeal Court at Westminster, upheld the verdict that a Town Hall or Offices could not be built in the park, but allowed the Corporation to build "a free conservatory, a free museum, and free library".

A competition to design the new building was won by local architects J. & T. Tillman, and their design was put into effect by

Cost of running a museum in 1868	
The estimate of expenses for the half-year ending 26 September 1868	
Rent	25. 0. 0
Cleaning, heating, lighting	11. 2. 0
Salaries, Curator & Attendant	37. 15. 0
Cases etc. joinery work	40. 0. 0
Stuffing	5. 0. 0
Purchase of specimens	50. 0. 0

The Museum from the air in the 1920s. Possibly a winter scene with snow on the ground.

Allison the builders at a cost of £11,700 for the museum and £2,000 for the Winter Gardens. When built, the new Museum, Library and Winter Gardens was the largest Civic building in Sunderland.

Many people believe that the foundation stone of the new building was laid by General Ulysses S. Grant, former President of the United States of America [it is an old curator's joke that Sunderland was the first museum in Britain to be Grant-aided]. However, Grant was merely *present* at the ceremony: the stone was laid by the Mayor Alderman Storey, on 24 September 1877, and the building officially opened by the Mayor, Councillor Robson, on November 6, 1879.

There was some controversy surrounding General Grant's visit. The Corporation spent £266 on, among other things, a fireworks display and a huge banquet, and this expenditure was challenged in the High Court. The court ruled that the council funds had been used illegally. The councillors eventually had to find the money out of their own pockets.

When the new museum was opened, a newspaper report in the *Daily Echo* commented:

"To those who remember the dingy rooms, formerly known as the Borough Museum, the effect of the new museum will appear quite a transformation and give the idea that a talismanic evolution from cobwebbed darkness to fairy brightness has occurred."

The evening reception for General Grant was reported in the *Sunderland Echo*.

Members of the public packed into the gallery and dress circle of the Victoria Hall and "gazed with never ending fascination" as civic leaders and their guests worked their way through the huge repast on the brilliantly decorated ground floor.

As an aid to digestion, the police band, under Mr Lax, played throughout the proceedings. The menu, supplied by Miss Lizzie Godley of the Palatine Hotel, consisted of goose pie, turkey poults, tongues in aspic, braised chicken, hams, ducklings, roast goose, roast turkey, braised beef, roast lamb, suckling pig, boar's head, goose pie in aspic, roast pork, collared veal, ham pies, pigeon pies, roast hare, grouse, partridge, raised pies, lobster, lobster salad, apple tarts, apricot tarts, raspberry tarts, Italian and lemon creams, jellies, blancmange, cream cheese and stilton cheese. Washed down with sherry, chablis, sauternes, champagne and claret.

THREE

THE ART GALLERY

The early collections of the Sunderland Museum did not include many paintings, and at first there was no need for a separate Art Gallery. Until at least 1880, it seems that the Corporation's collection of paintings was housed in the old Exchange News Room.

The most important early acquisition by the Corporation is probably *The Opening of Sunderland Docks*, which was commissioned from Mark Thompson in June 1854 at a cost of 30 guineas - probably the first painting ever to have been commissioned by a town council! Two other important acquisitions were drawings by Dante Gabriel Rossetti,

donated by the artist - at the suggestion of Thomas Dixon - to celebrate the opening of the new building.

When the Borough Road building was opened on November 7th 1879, the first floor contained a 'science and art room', divided into sections by curtains. It was planned to use this room for teaching purposes.

It was decided, in 1880 to turn the 'science and art room' into an Art Gallery. Although entry to the Museum Room was free, visitors to the Art Gallery were charged 6d on Mondays, Wednesdays and Fridays, and an extra penny to leave a walking stick or

Published in the 'Library Circular' in 1901, this is the earliest known photograph of the Art Gallery and shows the old style of hanging the pictures very closely spaced.

umbrella at the door. The money raised from admissions was used to buy paintings.

The artist John Ruskin designed a scheme of decoration for the new art gallery, but there is no evidence that the room was ever painted in the way that he suggested.

The collection expanded rapidly, and by 1898 the Corporation owned 104 paintings. The first catalogue of the Art Gallery was printed in 1886, priced at one penny. A reviewer in the *Daily Post* in 1905 commented:

"The Art Gallery has never been other than a Corporation Cinderella. One of the earliest reforms should be the abolition of the fee for admission. Another equally necessary reform is the overhaul of the collection with a view to the exclusion of worthless examples and palpable forgeries which are esteemed to be genuine. A report on the contents of the art gallery by an art expert would 'open the eyes' of the Museum and Library Committee."

A report on the state of the Art Gallery was prepared in 1906 by John Park A.R.E., and it contains some scathing comments. He recommended that several paintings should be discarded and others by artists then alive exchanged for higher quality work by the same artist. Most of the frames needed some repairs or regilding work done on them.

The fee to get into the Art Gallery, which seems to have varied over the years, was finally abolished in 1906. In that year the Art Gallery was decorated and the paintings cleaned.

Between 1904 and 1920 not a single painting was bought. An appeal in 1920 raised £400 and four modern paintings were purchased. The gallery relied on donations to purchase paintings up to 1939; from then an amount of £100 each year was allocated for the purchase of exhibits. In 1960 it increased to £400 and in 1964 became a cumulative fund which could

The Art Gallery, when the paintings were more widely spaced. Several of the paintings are still on permanent display, but the statue of an athlete struggling with a python (which was a plaster cast) was apparently discarded after being broken several decades ago.

Love Tunes the Shepherd's Reed

There was controversy in 1930 when the Art Gallery acquired 'Love Tunes the Shepherd's Reed' by Sunderland-born artist Richard Jack. The Libraries, Museums and Art Gallery Committee recommended its purchase, but some councillors objected that the painting had semi-nude figures in it, which made it "unsuitable for display in the Gallery". The artist replied, "To attack a picture like this in these days of scanty bathing costumes is absurd. The people who condemn that picture should wear paper bags on their heads when they go to the seaside lest they see something that might shock them." An appeal to the public, started by the *Sunderland Echo*, raised the £300 necessary to buy the painting.

be carried over from one financial year to the next. The Committee also agreed a new purchase policy which, with the advice of Dennis Farr from the Tate Gallery, led to the purchase of paintings by Anthony Gross, Edward Burra, Ruskin Spear, Robin Phillipson and Allen Jones.

The purchase of exhibits was aided by grants from the government purchase fund administered by the Victoria & Albert Museum, on behalf of the Museums & Galleries Commission. Major help has also been received over the years, particularly for the purchase of Sunderland pottery and glass, from the National Art Collections Fund. The Museum has also received several donations from the Contemporary Art Society.

Most of the paintings were removed from the building for safety in 1939 and stored

in Hexham, Langley Castle and Durham. When they returned after the war in 1945 the old system of double-hanging the paintings was abandoned, and they were hung in a single line on the walls.

As more paintings were being acquired and fewer were on display it was necessary to move some of them into a store. This pressure on space was alleviated with the opening of the new extension in 1964 when two additional galleries were available: a large one to be used for oil paintings and a smaller one (later closed) for watercolours. Both of the large art galleries were given new, suspended, ceilings that reduced the amount of daylight in the gallery, and natural light was totally excluded when the ceilings were replaced in the 1970s.

Dickinson Bequest

Many local Art Galleries were founded by wealthy benefactors who gave private collections of paintings or money. This is the case for Gateshead (Shipley Art Gallery), Newcastle (Laing Art Gallery), and Hartlepool (Gray Art Gallery). The wealthy shipbuilders and colliery owners of Sunderland did not follow their example, and there has never been any really large collection of paintings donated to Sunderland.

The biggest bequest to our Art Gallery was from John Dickinson, once head of an engineering firm, in 1908. In his will, Dickinson left 31 paintings to the Art Gallery. The press reported that "all are handsomely framed ...... landscapes predominate and in the collection Mr Dickinson favoured the English School and the modern masters. Altogether the works are of first-class merit. They greatly enrich the Gallery and form an addition to it of which the town has every reason to be proud while at the same time recognisant of the noble generosity of the donor".

A London critic, M.H. Shielmann, was more caustic: "from what I had heard I expected a more distinguished collection ... what a pity it is that these big provincial industrial magnates do not buy fine paintings; as it is they induce the public to adopt their own task and look at the second and third rate". It is, however, always easier to criticise than to achieve: Dickinson gave the town an important collection of paintings, Shielmann gave nothing except words.

Thomas Dixon and the Art Gallery

A major influence on the Art Gallery in its early years was Thomas Dixon. Dixon was born in Sunderland in 1831, and he earned his living in the town as a cork-cutter. He was a self-educated man and corresponded with several major literary figures and intellectuals, including Charles Dickens, John Ruskin, Dante Gabriel Rossetti and Thomas Carlyle. Dixon was an active member of the Museum Committee, and strongly supported the Art Gallery: he persuaded Rossetti to present two drawings for the opening of the new building, and Ruskin to draw up a design for the new gallery.

Right: Portrait of Thomas Dixon by Alphonse Legros. Painted in Sunderland on the day the Borough Road building opened in 1879, and presented to the Museum in 1881. "As Monsieur Legros proceeded to fill in the colour; every stroke of the brush seemed instinct with thought and in about an hour a telling and vigorous portrait had been produced in the very sight of the spectators".

The Art Gallery was radically altered in the 1960s, and the Victorian style was discarded in favour of a modern appearance. The suspended ceiling at first included translucent tiles that did not totally exclude daylight.

L.S. Lowry

Although normally associated with Salford, L.S. Lowry (1887-1976) had links with Sunderland for many years. He was a frequent visitor to the Museum and Art Gallery between 1960 and 1975 during the periods he spent at the Seaburn Hotel, when Sunderland became a second home for him. On one of his visits in November 1962 he was surprised to be greeted by name by James Wilson, the Principal Assistant Curator, who had worked at Salford Museums in the 1930s and 1940s and had met Lowry at a time when he was virtually unknown as an artist.

Lowry had several favourite works of art in the Art Gallery, which he asked to see if they were not on show: they were Hemy's *Old Sunderland*, the two drawings by

Rossetti and Dicksee's *Juliet*. He would say on looking at *Juliet* "if only I could paint like that".

Sunderland Museum and Art Gallery held one of Lowry's earliest one-man exhibitions in 1942, when the Art Editor of the *Sunderland Echo* wrote of the 'rare insight and brilliantly exact effort of the painting titled *Unemployed*'.

In 1966 the Arts Council held its first showing of its L.S. Lowry retrospective at Sunderland, and Lowry was present during the mounting of the exhibition. In 1989 the Museum held a major exhibition, *L.S. Lowry in the North East*. Generous loans of several works were made following this exhibition, and Sunderland now has the third largest public collection of Lowry's works outside of London.

L.S. Lowry with his painting 'The Pond' in the Art Gallery during preparations for the Arts Council retrospective exhibition in 1966.

Sunderland Art Gallery does not usually exhibit the more extreme examples of modern art: its strengths are in older oil paintings and watercolours, and there are other venues in Sunderland that specialise in contemporary art. In November 1977, however, the 'Response to Landscape' displaced the usual Sunderland Art Club annual show, and caused some controversy.

The *Sunderland Echo*'s reviewer was unsympathetic:

"Jos Mahon, Sculptor extraordinaire, has turned Sunderland Art Gallery into a piece of rugged Northern landscape. At least that's what his exhibition pamphlet says, but visitors could be forgiven for thinking they had accidentally encountered some art gallery alterations.

"And the *Echo* reporter who looked at the "Response to Landscape" couldn't decide whether the pile of museum chairs against the back wall was supposed to be part of it all.

"But Sunderland's answer to the Tate Gallery "bricks" is described by the Hexham-based artist himself as, "An interaction with location, not an attempt to compete with the vastness of nature. From daily, close contact with landscape, stems my feeling for shape and space, a concern with extension / the low and horizontal / linearity / ground hugging pieces. . . " says Mr Mahon."

A correspondent to the *Echo*, calling himself *Realist* was more forthright. His letter ended "Let junk end on the scrap heap of anarchistic ephemera".

The Museum Room changed little from 1879 until redevelopment in the 1960s. In later years, transport models were added to the natural history displays.

A mixed display of natural history and ethnography items on the balcony of the Museum Room in December 1960.

FOUR

THE MUSEUM, LIBRARY & WINTER GARDENS

The Museum

From 1879 until the 1960s the main gallery, called the Museum Room, was entered from the left side of the entrance hall. It was open to roof level and had a broad balcony on the first floor. In 1893 visitors got to this balcony via a spiral staircase, and the door leading out at first floor level was locked, but the staircase was later removed (it is not visible on any photographs) and there was access to the balcony from the Antiquities Room.

There was a broad range of specimens on display in the museum room, including lions, leopards, a tiger and polar bears,

models and casts of fish, antlers, British birds, foreign birds, sea shells, birds' eggs, fossils and minerals. In its earliest years it contained some human bones from archaeological sites and a mummified body from Peru, and later it was used to display models of trams, locomotives and locally-built ships.

In 1894, only fifteen years after it had been opened, the museum and library building was described as being 'totally inadequate', and plans were drawn up to build an extension between the present building and the Palatine (now the Mowbray) Hotel.

The Museum Room in June 1911. Most of the mammals still survive in the Museum's collections, and some are on loan to the Hancock Museum for display in 'Abel's Ark'. Wallace the Lion is to the bottom right of the picture.

The Museum Room, which had remained virtually unchanged for many years since 1879, was totally remodelled in the 1960s as a natural history display. The sparse style was very different to the old, crowded, Victorian displays.

The scheme never went ahead. In 1912 Andrew Carnegie, the American millionaire and philanthropist who had funded three branch libraries in Sunderland, was approached for funds for extending the building, but he replied quite reasonably that "it was about time that some of her wealthy citizens, or the people of Sunderland, did something for themselves in this need".

The displays in the Museum Room changed little from 1879 until the 1960s. As part of the development scheme a concrete floor was built across the old Museum Room at balcony level to divide it into a ground floor (Natural History) gallery, and first floor Art Gallery.

From 1964, the increased space for displays meant that separate galleries for natural history, geology, local and foreign archaeology, Sunderland pottery, glass,

The Local Wildlife display, built in 1977 portrays animals and plants in their natural setting, and was a move away from the older idea of having objects in glass cases. The conifer woodland is one of several dioramas.

The aquaria in the Local Wildlife display include some local saltwater species. The lobster tank is always popular.

ship models and local history could be created. The displays were all housed in large, airy galleries that presented a great contrast to the old crowded Victorian galleries.

A further stage in the development of the museum displays came in 1977 when the *Local Wildlife* gallery was opened. The gallery, based on an environmental theme, included dioramas showing animals and plants as they might look in their natural habitats, and tanks containing live animals that have proved to be among the most popular features of the museum. The gallery was considered to be trendsetting in its approach and has influenced others throughout the country. Other displays of that period were *Sunderland Pottery* (1979), *The North East Before Man* (1982), *Glassmaking on Wearside* (1984) and *The Sunderland Story* (1987). These

Bronze-framed glass case fronts are typical of the 1960s-style displays, all of which have subsequently been redeveloped. The Geology display was on the top floor of the new extension

displays placed more emphasis on the interpretation of the subject; previously stress had been on the design of single cases for each area. *The North East Before Man* was notable as it received financial support from B.P., the first time that a display in Sunderland had been sponsored.

A further new generation of displays started with *Lost Worlds* (1992) and continued with *...And Ships Were Born* (1993) and *Sunderland's Glorious Glass* (1994). These concentrated on creating a total environment, including hands-on exhibits and provision for visitors with disabilities, and have won several national awards.

Coal, the next major display, is due to open in the former lending library area in the Autumn of 1996. All of the major displays since 1993 have been designed by Redman Design Associates of Ilkley.

The staircase to the second floor is typical of the modern and stylish 1960s interior to the extension.

The Antiquities Room

The entrance Hall to the Museum is now open to the second storey, but before 1964 there was a floor at first-floor level, where a gallery contained a display of antiquities - ancient coins, pottery, objects from the prehistoric times, etc. This was called the Antiquities Room.

We know that in 1893 there were *only* antiquities in this room, in later years other objects were added to it. A photograph taken in 1960 shows that by then it also contained pottery, silver, prams and bicycles!

'... And Ships Were Born', a display about ships and shipbuilding on Wearside, was opened in 1993. It was the first of a new generation of displays at Sunderland Museum, the gallery includes an impressive audio-visual programme and a range of interactive exhibits in addition to the objects on display.

Robert Blair's article in *Antiquity* in 1893 (see Chapter 9) gives some interesting information about the Antiquities Room room, as well as a list of its contents. It did not form part of the 'Free Museum', and visitors were at one time charged to get into this room and the Art Gallery.

The Library

Sunderland Museum has shared a building with a library on two occasions in its history - in High Street West and in Borough Road - but they were two different libraries. The Public Library must be distinguished from the earlier, private, Subscription Library. The Public Libraries Act of 1850 allowed libraries to be run by town councils, supported by the rates, and Sunderland Public or Free Library was opened in 1858 in the Athenaeum. It was transferred to Borough Road in 1879, and shared the building with the museum for the next 116 years, moving to Fawcett Street in 1995.

Assistant Curator Marilyn Carr models the donation of a Victorian dress in one of the 'Period Room' displays in 1972.

Displays of Chinese ivories and glass in the Entrance Hall in 1960. The movable bronze-framed Edmonds cases have been used for temporary displays for several decades, and are still in use.

The walrus at the foot of the stairs from the entrance hall, leading to the Antiquities Room and Art Gallery, in December 1960. The staircase was moved during the 1960s development scheme.

The Subscription Library, unlike the Subscription Museum, never passed into public hands. It continued to operate as a private concern for many years, separate from the Public Library. It moved to Fawcett Street in 1878, to the glass-domed building that now houses the National Westminster Bank, and eventually closed in 1938.

The Winter Gardens

The Winter Gardens was built in 1879 on the south side of the museum, and visitors could enter either from the museum side or from the park. The Sunderland Echo gave details of the structure in 1879, as follows: The roof was constructed of curved T-section iron ribs, supported at intervals on metal columns, and glazed with rough plate glass. The dome in the centre gave the conservatory a finished and elegant appearance. The front and sides were built of pitch pine, and glazed with sheet glass. The ventilators on the roof ran the full length of the buildings. The heating was

The Corporation's Library shared the building with the Museum and Art Gallery from 1879 until 1995. In the early years there was no public access to the bookshelves. Visitors consulted a catalogue and asked for the books of their choice.

The Library in 1960. Visitors can be seen browsing among the books, although access to the top shelves must have been difficult. Problems of lack of space were eased when the Lending Library was developed in the new extension scheme.

by low-pressure hot-water apparatus.... On the floor of the conservatory beds were laid out for plants, and between these were footpaths. Under the footpaths, which were of iron grating, was the heating apparatus... under the dome was a small pond for goldfish, with an ornamental fountain in the centre.

A Winter Gardens is specially designed to display plants, whereas a conservatory can be used for several purposes and doesn't always have plants in it. When opening the Borough Road building in 1879, the Mayor of Sunderland said that, "The conservatory is not what I expected it to be. I thought it was a place where the public could enjoy themselves, and have a little music and such like. It has, however, taken more the form of a winter garden. I hope it will answer, but if it does not it will not cost much to clear away the shrubs and make it a place of recreation and amusement for the people rather than a mere show place."

With its luxuriant plants, goldfish pond and live birds, the Winter Gardens must have been a place of wonder in its early days. There was a parrot (a Turquoise-fronted Parrot, *Amazona aestiva*) that lived there for years, and used to shout out to visitors "What time is it?". When it died, the bird was stuffed and put on display in the museum, but it probably deteriorated and was discarded many years ago.

By the 1930s, the Winter Gardens building was thought to be too small for the number of visitors using it, and the structure was in

The Winter Gardens in 1892. The terrace by the lake has long been a popular site for family recreation.

There were plans to demolish the Winter Gardens in the 1930s, but its fate was finally sealed by this bomb damage on April 16th 1941.

poor condition. In a scheme proposed to the Corporation on January 10th 1934, the museum's Director Charlton Deas proposed knocking it down and building a museum extension on the back of the building with a Floral Hall in the park.

Although nothing came of the Corporation's scheme, the days of the Winter Gardens were indeed numbered. On April 16th 1941 it was so severely damaged by an exploding parachute mine dropped by a German bomber that it had to be demolished. On another night four incendiary bombs fell on the Museum and four on the Winter Gardens and the Janitor's wife and her two daughters used buckets of sand to extinguish the fires, saving the building. Twenty-three years later, a new extension would be completed in the place of the old Winter Gardens.

The Extension Scheme

For over twenty years a scar remained on the back of the building where the Winter Gardens had once been. In 1959 it was decided to do something about it. There was to be no new Winter Gardens or Floral Hall, but an extension was built - similar in scope to the scheme proposed in the 1930s - to provide space for a lending library, two floors of museum galleries (each of 5,000 square feet) and office space for the museum and library staff.

This scheme, completed in 1964, was more than just an extension to the building, for the interior was extensively remodelled. A floor was put into the Natural History Gallery (at the level of the old balcony) in order to create an extra Art Gallery, and the entrance hall was changed by having the first floor taken out and a new staircase put in. For the first time, the museum also had its own tea room.

Tom Shaw, who was Deputy Director in 1959 and then Director from 1960-73, recalled how the new extension came about:

"Strangely enough it all started by the Borough Treasurer casting his eyes on the 'Shack' in Fawcett Street, adjacent to the Town Hall, where the Children's Library and the Reading Rooms had been housed temporarily since about 1910. He wanted accommodation for the Motor Taxation department which was to come under his control. We were offered £38,000 for a scheme to extend on part of the Winter Gardens site, to the south of the existing library, as a portico extension to the library and to house the children's sections and reading rooms. It was to be a kind of pre-fab extension. Hardly had we got the plans ready for this when we were asked (to our delight and surprise) to design a major scheme taking over all of the Winter Gardens site - a three-storey extension for both Library, Museum and Art Gallery. This became the £250,000 scheme".

The money to complete this major scheme became available at the last moment and in order to qualify for the approval by the Ministry of Housing and Local Government of the capital expenditure, plans had to be completed within a few weeks.

Tom Shaw also recalls that the Carnegie United Kingdom Trust were approached to give a grant. He subsequently felt that more than the grant of £750 was spent in providing reports and hospitality for experts who reported on the project to the trustees.

The extension led to an increase in museum staff from one Senior Assistant Curator and one Museum Assistant, to a total of six - Principal Assistant Curator, Senior Assistant Curator, Assistant Curator, two Museum Assistants and a Handyman. Tom Shaw "felt that more work was put into assessing enquiries and displaying the collections than at any time during the previous 75 years. The transformation was magnificent

The site of the demolished Winter Gardens before construction of the new extension got underway.

The new extension being built in the early 1960s on the site of the demolished Winter Gardens.

and had rave notices locally and nationally. Visitor figures more than doubled".

The extension was designed by Sunderland's Borough Architect, Harvey Bishop, and the main contractors were D & J Ranken Ltd. The building and refurbishment work cost £218,000. The new Museum and Library building was gradually completed between 1962 and 1964, and Her Majesty Queen Elizabeth the Queen Mother came to Sunderland to open the building officially in 1964.

In the spirit of the 1960s, the extension was designed to look modern, in what is sometimes called *Festival of Britain* style. Although at times criticised for being out of keeping with the old museum building, it is considered a good example of its type. The south of the building features the

corporation crest, and a covered walkway with decorative tiles by W. Hudspith from Sunderland College of Art.

Inside the building, the design of the newly remodelled galleries was also modern but plain. A photograph of the Natural History gallery at that time shows it looking bright and clean, perhaps almost too clean and antiseptic in appearance.

The Art Gallery space doubled in size, and there was an extra small gallery for watercolours. The exhibition space for the museum tripled. The first floor of the extension housed displays on local industries such as glassmaking, pottery, shipbuilding, engineering and rope-making, and displays of coins, medals and silver. The second floor was devoted to history, archaeology and geology.

Museum & Library, Sunderland

Winter Gardens (Interior) Sunderland

Interior of Winter Gardens, Sunderland

The Museum and Winter Gardens were popular subjects for postcards of Sunderland at the turn of the century.

The Walrus and the Carpenter
Walked on a mile or so,
And then they rested on a rock
Conveniently low:
And all the little Oysters stood
And waited in a row.

Walrus and Carpenter

This charming watercolour was on display for many years in the foyer of Sunderland Museum, and promoted the legend that our walrus inspired Lewis Carroll to write *The Walrus and the Carpenter*. However, the poem was published in 1871 and the museum did not acquire the walrus until 1874 so there can be no truth in the story.

H.M. Queen Elizabeth the Queen Mother opens the new extension in June 1964, talking to (left) the Mayor of Sunderland Alderman R. Wilkinson, (centre) Councillor Ernest Joice, Chairman of the Libraries, Museums and Art Gallery Committee, and (right) Tom Shaw, the Museum's Director.

View across Mowbray Park lake towards the new extension.

Artist's impression of the proposed Sunderland Pottery display.

FUTURE PLANS

1996 sees the Museum's development continue with the opening of a further display - *Coal* - in the former library area. To follow the *Coal* display, plans have been drawn up for a scheme that will transform the Museum and which include the following:

- A new entrance at the corner of Burdon Road and Borough Road

- Public lifts to the first and second floors.

- Public toilets

- A new, larger, cafe in the former reference library area

- A new shop

- An education / lecture area in the present Natural History gallery

- New displays including natural history, textiles, Sunderland archaeology, history, pottery, geology and art.

- Improved storage areas

- Replacement of boilers, heating and ventilation equipment to provide a stable environmental control for exhibits.

The scheme is being submitted to the National Lottery Heritage Fund for 75% of the £5,000,000 required.

The largest work of art in the gallery, at 12 ft by 8 ft, this painting is unusual in showing a football match. It may be the earliest surviving painting showing Association Football action and is an important facet of the links between Sunderland Museum & Art Gallery and the local community. It was commissioned by Sunderland AFC in 1895 and shows a match played on January 2nd at the Newcastle Road ground - the club's home venue before Roker Park - between Sunderland and Aston Villa. The painting was cleaned and the frame restored in 1994 with the aid of financial assistance from the SAFC Supporters' Association, and is on loan to us from Sunderland AFC.

Large pink lustre teapot, probably made at Scott's Southwick Pottery in the 1860s. The transfer decoration includes a print of the rebuilt Wearmouth Bridge of 1859. The teapot was bequested to the Museum by Lord Stephen Ross of Newport in 1993.

Studies of a head by Dante Gabriel Rossetti (1828-1882)
The chalk drawings were presented by the artist in 1879, and it seems that Thomas Dixon used his influence to obtain them for the Art Gallery. The figures are from Rossetti's oil painting *Astarte Syriaca* which is in the Manchester City Art Gallery.

Snow on Tunstall Hills by David Robertson (1879-1952).
Robertson was a Sunderland artist who specialised in landscape and animal subjects. This local scene is one of the popular local paintings in the Art Gallery

The silver gun, a memorial to the 197 men of the 125th Anti-Tank Regiment, R.A. who died in action or as Japanese prisoners of war.

The 125th Anti-Tank Regiment, R.A.

The 125th Anti-Tank Regiment of the Royal Artillery was initially a Territorial Army unit with its headquarters in Sunderland. Raised early in 1939, after initial training the regiment was shipped to Singapore. Their transport was attacked by Japanese planes on arrival at Singapore and the men were forced to abandon ship, leaving behind all their personal belongings and equipment. 62% of the men arrived in Singapore suffering from burns.

Ten days after landing the British forces in Singapore surrendered, and the regiment was taken into a captivity that lasted three and a half years. After terrible suffering in the Japanese Prisoner of War camps, the survivors were released in August 1945 and shipped home.

The Silver Memorial Gun was presented to the regiment in 1951 by Colonel Sir Robert Chapman in honour of its officers and men, and is on loan to the museum. Four plaques on the base record the names of the 197 men who died in action or as prisoners of war. The gun assumed a special significance in 1995, the 50th anniversary of the release of the survivors of the Regiment from Prisoner of War camps in the Far East. It was the centrepiece of the service held at the Museum and was also featured in an item about VJ Day on television on August 9th. James Cranmer, whose five brothers joined the 125th (three of whom died as a result of the war), was shown discussing the Memorial Gun in the Museum with Bill Hamilton. As a result of this item on TV the Museum was contacted by the relations of several members of the Regiment who had died in the Far East.

FIVE

SOME EXHIBITS AND LEGENDS

Wallace the Lion

Wallace the lion may look a little worse for wear, but this is hardly surprising as he is over 120 years old. For many years, he has been one of the 'stars' of Sunderland Museum. He has been the favourite of the people of Sunderland since the 1870s, and even now, we often hear parents saying to their children "come on upstairs and we'll see the lion".

When he was alive, Wallace travelled with Mander's Menagerie, a 'wild beast show'. In 1868 when the Menagerie was at Sunderland he mauled his trainer, a man called Martini Macomo. Although badly bitten and crushed, Macomo survived until two years later, when the Menagerie was again visiting Sunderland, he caught a fever and died in the Palatine Hotel. He is buried in Bishopwearmouth Cemetery.

Wallace lived until the 18th of February 1875, when he died at Warrington at the age of 13. He was sent to the taxidermist William Yellowly at South Shields, who stuffed him.

Sunderland Museum bought Wallace from Yellowly in 1879, and he has been on display here ever since, except for occasional 'outings' - for instance in 1918 he took part in the peace parade marking the end of World War I, when he toured Sunderland in an open-topped cart standing beside a lady dressed as Britannia.

Blind children handling stuffed animals and sitting on Wallace the Lion as part of Charlton Deas's programme of activities in 1913.

Sunderland Pottery

Pottery was made on Wearside from about 1720. In the second half of the 18th Century its manufacture was transformed from a rural craft to a mass production industry. For much of the 19th Century Sunderland exported large quantities of earthenware to the Continent. However, this trade greatly diminished during the last three decades of the century when the industry went into decline, and by 1900 only three potteries were still working.

The best known products of the Sunderland potteries are the creamware, pink lustre and transfer-printed wares, particularly the jugs and mugs decorated with transfer-prints of the 1796 Wear Bridge. Many other types of earthenware were also produced on Wearside, including brown earthenware, slipware, marbleware, yellow transfer printed brownware, cream-coloured and yellow-glazed ware.

There has been a distinct change in attitude towards Sunderland pottery over the years. At one time pottery from Sunderland was mostly regarded as everyday, cheap-and-cheerful ware that hardly merited a place in a museum.

Although there were some major acquisitions, such as the Scott (1897) and Rowland Burdon (1945) collections, even in 1960 there was only a tiny display of local pottery in the Museum, on show in the Antiquarian Room.

The major change came in 1964, with the opening of the new extension. There was now much more room available, which allowed the curators to get more of the collection out of the stores. At the same time, Sunderland pottery came to be treated as items of value: in effect, as antiques rather than junk.

The museum has played a part in this change, not only by means of the permanent display

Local (Ball's Pottery) pieces celebrating Jack Crawford, the Hero of the Battle of Camperdown. Although said to have used a Marlin Spike to nail the colours to the mast, he is often shown (as here) using the butt of a pistol as a hammer. The plate is on permanent display at the Museum, the jug belongs to a private collector.

and temporary exhibitions, but through several books and booklets: *The Potteries of Sunderland and District* (1951, 1961) *Rhymes and Mottoes on Sunderland Pottery* (1960); *The Potteries of Sunderland and District* (1968); *Sunderland Ware, The Potteries of Wearside* (1973) and *Sunderland Pottery* (1984).

The largest collection of Sunderland pottery given to the museum, known as the Rowland Burdon Collection, comprises about 120 items. It was presented to the museum in 1945 by the Hon. Mrs Walter Sclater-Booth of Castle Eden, daughter of Colonel Rowland Burdon. By acquiring this collection, Sunderland Museum was able to mount a large display of local pottery, and this in turn changed people's opinions of Sunderland Ware.

The Museum now has about 500 pieces of Sunderland pottery. An important donation came in 1897 from Scott's Pottery, following the closure of the factory. This collection is most important because it gives us a collection of pieces that we *know* came from Sunderland, as it is often very difficult to decide precisely where a piece was made!

There are currently 20 cases of Sunderland - and other - pottery on display in the museum, providing a very important resource for the growing band of people who collect Sunderland Ware.

Sunderland Glass

Glassmaking is one of Sunderland's oldest industries, established by the Sunderland Company of Glassmakers in the 1690s. It has continued to be of importance up to the present day. During the 18th Century the glass of Tyneside and Wearside came to dominate the London market, and glassmaking on Wearside continued to expand until the middle of the 19th Century. A rapid decline followed, leading to the closure of most of the leading firms by the 1920s.

There were three main areas of production on Wearside: bottles, window-glass and tableware. At one time, Sunderland had the biggest bottle-making factory in the world, the Ayre's Quay Bottle Works.

The Museum has a particularly fine collection of the tablewares. These range from superb

Some items from the Londonderry Service.

quality blown pieces with cut and engraved decoration such as the Londonderry Service and the large engraved Victorian rummers, to the cheap and cheerful pressed glass that was produced in great quantities (particularly from the mid-19th Century up to the 1930s). In 1921 Pyrex was first made in Britain, by the Sunderland glassmakers James A. Jobling and Co. It is still being made in Sunderland today.

As with Sunderland Pottery, the art world at one time had little interest in Sunderland Glass. For many years it was held in little esteem by collectors, and indeed some critics refused to believe that the fine-quality Londonderry Service could have been made in such a place as Sunderland.

The changing point in people's ideas of Sunderland Glass came about in 1964, with the space newly available in the extension allowing the development of a display about local glass. A booklet about the local glass industry was also published by the Museum (*The Glass Industry of Tyne and Wear, Part 1: Glassmaking on Wearside*, 1979), but is no longer in print.

Among the early acquisitions related to the glass industry were certificates and medallions given to the Museum by Hartley's in 1894, and local glass has been collected over the years. The most important collection of glass in the museum is 160 pieces of the Londonderry Service, a table service made between 1819 and 1824 by the Wear Flint Glass company for the Marquess of Londonderry, at a price of 2,000 guineas. The service was bought for Sunderland Museum in 1986 for £47,500 with the aid of grants from the Museums and Galleries Commission, the Victoria and Albert Museum Purchase Grant Fund and the National Art Collections Fund.

The glass display was redeveloped in 1994. The display highlights Sunderland Glass and includes the Londonderry Service and rummers as well as pressed glass. A continuing attraction is the case containing novelty items, like the glass walking sticks.

The Fossil Tree

The fossil tree, 6ft long and 5ft in circumference, has long been a favourite with visitors. A *Sigillaria* species from the Carboniferous period, it is one of three trees found in 1840 at North Biddick Colliery. The tree is one of the oldest exhibits in the museum: not only has it been on display for over 150 years, but it lay underground for over 300 million!

The tree grew in the warm humid swamps that covered the whole of the north of England in the Carboniferous period. As the plants in the swamp died they became buried under other sediments, and turned into coal. Some of the plants and animals (like this tree) were preserved as fossils among the coal.

The Log Boat

The log boat on display on the first floor of the museum was found on the river bottom at Offerton Haugh in 1888 by the diver Harry Watts (whose diving suit is also on display). It is made of oak, 3.5m. long, and is said to have contained human bones when found, but there may have been confusion with another log boat (also from Offerton) found in 1880.

Log boats were made over a long period, from the Bronze age to the Middle Ages, and it is not possible to date them by style. Because this boat has been treated with preservatives, radiocarbon dating is not possible, so we will probably never know how old it is.

James Wilson's bequest of Silver

Alderman James Wilson, owner of several local cinemas, built up a large collection of silver items, and on his death in 1947 it was bequeathed to Sunderland Museum. There were 204 pieces, ranging in date from 1559 to 1806, including chalices, salvers, tankards, cups, spoons, candlesticks, porringers, tea caddies and other fine examples of English domestic silver. The collection was valued in 1947 at between £4,000 and £5,000. The collection is not currently on public display.

Activities for blind children organised by Charlton Deas: experiencing the log boat.

The Backhouse Collection

Edward Backhouse Jr was a member of a wealthy family of Quaker bankers. He is remembered as perhaps the greatest philanthropist ever to have lived in Sunderland. Edward Backhouse greatly enriched the museum during his lifetime by giving specimens for the displays. His own collection was one of the largest in private hands anywhere in Britain, the cabinets, when laid end-to-end, were 85 metres long. Backhouse died in 1879, and in 1907 the collection was given to Sunderland Museum: it included British and foreign butterflies, shells, fossils (including some fine fossil fish), birds, flint implements and other archaeological finds, corals, African weapons, paintings, Fijian weapons and coins. We still have his collection in Sunderland Museum, much of it kept in the stores.

C.T. Trechmann's collection

Whilst there have been some major donations to Sunderland Museum, from Edward Backhouse and John Dickinson for instance, in 1966 Sunderland missed an opportunity to acquire another very important private collection.

Dr Charles T. Trechmann (1885- 1965) was a member of a family of wealthy industrialists with interests in the Hartlepool area. With very wide interests and the money to back them up, Dr Trechmann was able to build up extensive and varied collections. His house was said to have been stuffed full from attic to cellar with all kinds of collectors' items: there was a coin collection valued at £40,000, bronzes from Benin, Japanese netsuke, gold figurines, archaeological material, fossils, minerals, insects, a large collection of books and journals, etc., etc.

In his will, Trechmann offered the collection to Sunderland Museum, together with a legacy of £5,000 to build an extension to house it. Sunderland Council turned down the offer, partly because the new extension had only just opened, and partly because £5,000 would not be enough to build a new wing. Collections of New Zealand ethnographic material and Egyptian antiquities were sent to the Royal Scottish Museum in Edinburgh, and it took several removal vans to take the natural history collections and books to the Natural History Museum in London. Although Sunderland

Museum did not acquire the whole of Dr Trechmann's bequest, there are important geological, biological and archaeological items, antiquities and Oriental works of art in our collections which were donated by him.

Colonel Lilburne's Boots

Colonel Lilburne's Boots are among the few survivors of the Sunderland Subscription Museum, and were listed in the catalogue of 1825.

The Lilburne family was at one time one of the wealthiest and most powerful in Sunderland. Colonel John Lilburne, also known as 'Free-born John' (1618-1657), was a puritan and stood for freedom of the individual against the state. He had a short but active life, and died at the age of 39. He was sentenced at the age of 19 to be whipped through the streets of London, pilloried and imprisoned for life; released; fought in the civil war on the side of Parliament; fell out with Cromwell; was exiled, and returned to live out his last days as a Quaker. He is famous for publishing many political pamphlets.

We don't know why somebody kept his boots, but they were presented to the Subscription Museum by Thomas Richardson.

Some museum legends:

The Walrus and the Carpenter

Even if visitors know little else about Sunderland Museum, they know that there is a walrus on display that inspired Lewis Carroll to write his poem about "The Walrus and the Carpenter"(see page 29).

For many years there was a charming painting of the Walrus, Carpenter and oysters on display beside the Walrus, and part of the poem:

> The Walrus and the Carpenter
> Walked on a mile or so,
> And then they rested on a rock
> Conveniently low:
> And all the little Oysters stood
> and waited in a row

Lewis Carroll - whose real name was Charles Dodgson - published the poem in 1871 in his book *Through the Looking Glass*. About this time he was staying with his cousins, the Misses Wilcox at Whitburn, and the story goes that he was inspired by the carpenters building the wooden ships and by the Walrus on display in the museum. The oysters supposedly came into the poem because he had seen oyster fishermen at Whitburn.

Although it is a good story, it is not true. Recent research has shown that the Walrus was not given to the museum until three years after the poem had been published.

The Walrus was presented to the Museum in November 1874 by Captain Wiggins, a sailor who pioneered the trade route between Britain and Siberia. The Walrus was probably brought back to Britain as a flat skin, as the curator was asked to have it stuffed. It stood in the Museum for many years, at the foot of the stairs from the entrance hall. By 1965 it had deteriorated very badly and the body was discarded, only the head being kept. There is another story from that time, that the body was stuffed with coal!

In 1986 the head was given a complete overhaul. It was very dirty and greasy, and was cleaned, degreased, coloured, and then fitted with over 200 individually-made nylon whiskers: the old "whiskers" were found to have been made out of feather quills.

Jack Crawford's Heart

There is a legend that Jack Crawford's heart used to be on display in Sunderland Museum. In 1947, when Charlton Deas wrote an article for the *Sunderland Echo* about museum fables, he stated that a heart "reputed to be Jack Crawford's" had been on display when the Museum was housed in the Athenaeum.

Jack Crawford "The Hero of Camperdown" was one of Sunderland's local heroes. Born on Pottery Bank in 1775, he either joined - or

The Walrus in 1962.

was press-ganged into - the navy as a boy, and in 1797 was on Admiral Duncan's ship *Venerable* when it fought against the Dutch at the battle of Camperdown off the coast of Holland. During the battle the *Venerable*'s colours were shot away six times and replaced. A seventh time, they landed on deck together with part of the mast. Jack Crawford climbed the mast, amid heavy fire, and nailed the colours to the topgallant head using a marlin spike as a hammer. This seems to have been the origin of the phrase "nail your colours to the mast"

On leaving the Navy Jack Crawford returned to Sunderland where he became a keelman. Unfortunately, he was one of the earliest victims of the cholera epidemic of 1831. A monument still stands in Mowbray Park, showing Jack nailing the colours to the mast, and there is a small display about him in the museum that includes a medal given to him by the people of Sunderland.

We don't know where and when the story originated about Jack Crawford's heart being on display, but there appears to be no truth in it at all. Not only would most people consider it rather gruesome to have a recently deceased human heart on display in a museum, but it is doubtful that the Crawford family would want to see part of their relative on public show. Also, Jack Crawford died of Cholera, and few people would want to handle the remains of a victim of such a virulent disease.

In his *Echo* article, Charlton Deas recorded that several items of morbid interest had been brought in to him by members of the public over the years, including "the door bolt that caused the Victoria Hall disaster".

The balcony of the Museum Room was used as space for temporary exhibitions for many years. The cases were masked off and exhibits mounted in front of them. Here, a school party inspects a display of drawings from London schools.

The balcony of the Museum Room in 1957, looking towards the Antiquities Room. This area was floored over to provide space for a second Art Gallery as part of the 1960s development scheme.

SIX

EXHIBITIONS

Displays and Exhibitions

Museums generally have on show a range of permanent displays and temporary exhibitions. A temporary exhibition is mounted in a gallery for a few weeks or months - in Sunderland there is a programme of several different exhibitions every year. A permanent display might occupy a gallery for several decades. The fact that 'permanent' displays do eventually change surprises some people, who come in to see something they remember from their childhood and are disappointed to find that it is no longer on display.

A balance has to be drawn between exhibitions and displays. On the one hand there are complaints that the displays 'haven't changed for years', and on the other hand that the exhibitions don't stay long enough - people sometimes ask to see an exhibition that came to the museum several years ago and was here for only a few months.

Temporary exhibitions

Sunderland museum has a long history of putting on temporary exhibitions. The general policy of showing loan exhibitions each Spring was instigated as early as the 1880s. These proved so popular that the North Eastern Railway Company was asked to arrange special trains during the holidays to enable people to visit the

A wartime exhibition, in 1941, in the Art Gallery on 'Safety of Life at Sea'. Notice that at that time the paintings were not removed from the walls when temporary exhibitions were on show.

A temporary wartime exhibition in the entrance hall. The tail of a leopard, just visible in a case on the far right, was part of a display which was presented by the Earl of Durham.

exhibition. Exhibits were then regularly available on loan from the South Kensington Museum (the forerunner of the Victoria & Albert Museum), and later from a number of institutions and societies. Between 1906 and 1939 under the directorship of Charlton Deas there were 200 exhibitions, usually on an artistic theme and involving paintings, drawings, etchings and photographs.

There were special exhibitions on military subjects during both world wars, part of their purpose being to maintain morale but they also raised money for the war effort. Between 1914 and 1918, £1,370 was raised for various war charities - the Belgian Relief Fund, D.L.I. Prisoners of War, Canadian War Memorials, Naval War Charities and the Austrian "Save the Children" fund.

Between 1939 and 1945 there was a series of war-related exhibitions and activities,

including "War Weapons Week" in November 1940, "Warship Week" February 1942, "Wings for Victory" May 1943 and "Salute the Soldier" June 1944.

"Wings for Victory" was part of a Sunderland-wide campaign to raise £1,250 to support the R.A.F. Although arranged by the museum's Director, the display was on show in The Rink and not in the museum. The other displays were held either in the Art Gallery or in the entrance hall.

Because of lack of space to store the paintings, in the early days they were not taken off the walls when a temporary exhibition was in the gallery: nowadays the gallery is completely emptied between shows.

There has been a long tradition of exhibitions by two local organisations, the

Sunderland Photographic Association, who mounted their *Jubilee Exhibition* in 1938, and Sunderland Art Club, which held its first exhibition in the Art Gallery in 1945. Both groups have annual exhibitions in the Art Gallery.

In the 1960s and 1970s several major exhibitions were organised that involved bringing together items from other institutions. These included *Durham Cathedral Topographical Prints* in 1969, and *Bede, Wearmouth and Christian Culture*, organised as part of the

Wearmouth Festival in 1973 and involving the loan of important Anglo-Saxon manuscripts from the British Library.

The scale of temporary exhibitions increased notably with *The Spectacular Career of Clarkson Stansfield* in 1979. This exhibition of the Sunderland-born artist's paintings and theatrical work involved getting loans from public collections and it was shown subsequently in Germany. A substantial catalogue was published to accompany the exhibition. Further exhibitions on the same scale have

In addition to the permanent displays, there are several temporary exhibitions each year. The 'Mingei' exhibition in 1991 included an impressive collection of items brought on tour from the Japanese Folk Crafts Museum in Tokyo.

'The Changing Face of Wearside', on display from 1979 to 1982, showed the history of Sunderland through paintings, prints, maps and photographs.

been *L.S. Lowry in the North East* (1989) and *The Art of Glass*, the Museum's major contribution to *The Year of Visual Arts* in 1996, which included loans from European and Royal collections. Some other exhibitions created in-house by Tyne and Wear Museums have involved fewer loans but had an equal impact on visitor numbers, include *Buildings of Sunderland 1814-1914* (1979), *The World of Toys* (1992), *Saints and a Sinner* (1994) and *Claws* (1995).

In recent years Sunderland has continued to benefit from 'Masterpiece' loans from the National collections, including *From Turner's Studio* (1990) and Constable's *The Opening of Waterloo Bridge* (1995). In 1998 the museum will be displaying Drouet's *Madame Pompadour* and Lawrence's *Queen Charlotte* from the National Gallery. These major loan

exhibitions always draw large numbers of visitors to the museum.

In the last decade there has been a trend towards having fewer, but larger, temporary exhibitions. Whereas in the past the exhibition comprised a set of paintings or photographs that was circulated to many of the art galleries around the country, several of the most successful exhibitions in recent years have been designed in-house - *Dolls, Saints and a Sinner* and *Toys*, for instance, or they have been hired in from outside but heavily supplemented with our own material - such as *The Barbarians!* and *Exploitation Earth*.

Almost all of the temporary exhibitions have a programme of related activities such as drop-in craft workshops in the museum, or talks and guided walks.

Temporary Exhibitions, 1992-1996

8 February - 26 April 1992
The Barbarians came from Scunthorpe Museum and was greatly enhanced by important Celtic exhibits from the Royal Museum of Scotland, our own collections and elsewhere. Activities included weaving, corn grinding, making pottery and jewellery, storytelling and outdoor activities.

9-31 May 1992
Sunderland Photographic Association

16 June - 12 July 1992
The Kent Master Collection included 16th-19th century European drawings from Kent city council's collections

25 July - 16 September 1992
The World of Dolls attracted over 34,000 visitors to see this display of dolls and dolls' houses. Popular activities included workshops, storytelling sessions and two photographic sessions

19 September - 11 October 1992
Sunderland Art Club

24 October 1992 - 10 January 1993
New City Landscape / Women in Westminster comprised two photographic exhibitions: Roland Boyes, MP for Houghton and Washington, showed portraits of women in the Houses of Parliament, and Isabela Jedrzejczyk's photographs depicted Sunderland's changing industrial landscape.

16 January - 28 March 1993
A Fresh Look: a selection by Nerys Johnson of paintings from the collections of Middlesbrough Art Gallery. Activities included school workshops, workshops aimed at people with disabilities and a competition to name one of Nerys Johnson's own pictures on display.

3 - 25 April 1993
Sunderland Photographic Association

22 May - 12 June 1993
Wildlife Photographer of the Year is an ever-popular touring exhibition of the winners of the international competition for wildlife photographers.

25 June - 8 August 1993
The Staithes Group was organised by Nottingham Castle Museum, and showed the work of some of the most influential members of the North Yorkshire artists' colony.

25 August - 31 October 1993
BP Re-Vision came on tour from the Greenwich Citizens Gallery, and encouraged people to use all of their senses in experiencing the contemporary art exhibits.

16 July - 3 October 1993
The World of Toys was the first showing of a highly successful exhibition that subsequently toured other venues in Tyne & Wear. It featured toys from the 1890s to 1990s, and the computer games and soft play area proved particularly popular.

6-25 November 1993
Sunderland Art Club

3 December 1993 - 6 March 1994
One for the Pot featured over 100 teapots from the Twining Teapot Gallery at Norwich Castle Museum, as well as a 'tea sniffing box' and related events such as a Mad Hatter's tea Party, Tea Tasting Session and Teapots Roadshow.

26 March - 9 May 1994
Exploitation Earth was a small touring exhibition hired from Glasgow Museums and enhanced by a wide variety of material from our own collections - paintings as well as natural history objects.
21 June - 2 October 1994

Saints and a Sinner traced the history and activities of the Backhouse family, leading bankers, Quakers and philanthropists in North-East England, and took a look at their many interests.

16 October - 6 November 1994
Sunderland Art Club marked the 50th anniversary of the club, and included a special section of paintings by founder members.

12 November 1994 - 8 January 1995
Minnie the Minx and the Bash Street Kids

Images in one of Sunderland Photographic Association's annual exhibitions in the Art Gallery.

was taken on hire from the Harris Museum Preston, and celebrated 40 years of Minnie, and other characters drawn by Leo Baxendale. A classroom for visitors to read comics, and a play area proved great attractions.

28 January - 19 March 1995
Constable's "The opening of Waterloo Bridge" came to Sunderland from the Tate Gallery, as part of a tour to four venues. Paintings celebrating local river events were used to supplement the display.

1-23 April 1995
Sunderland Photographic Association

29 April - 9 July 1995
Simpson's Sunderland 1930-1950 looked at the work of Herbert Simpson, who taught at the Sunderland School of Art in the 1930s and 1940s, and included works by his colleagues and pupils.

22 July - 15 October 1995
Claws, on tour from the Hancock Museum, was an exhibition about the cat family. It featured a full size growling sabre-tooth tiger, and many examples of the 38 species of felines along with several hands-on interactives. A wide variety of family activities were organised in conjunction with the exhibition. This was the most popular exhibition ever at Sunderland Museum.

21 October - 12 November 1995
Sunderland Art Club

18 November 1995 - 26 February 1996
Time Please! showed the history of Sunderland's pubs and the local temperance movement. It included carved pub signs, pub furniture, bottles and tankards from pubs, as well as temperance banners, posters and pottery. There was also the opportunity to play pub games ranging from shove ha'penny to pool.

SEVEN

EDUCATION & AWARDS

Education

Education in its broadest sense was one of the reasons why Sunderland Corporation took over the museum in 1846, and it has remained one of the major objectives to the present day. There was at first only limited working with schools, colleges and adult groups, but this has been an increasing feature of the museum during the 20th century.

Robert Cameron, one of the museum's early honorary curators, expressed the importance of museums being related to the curriculum for schools in a paper he gave to the Museums Association conference in 1890.

Although Charlton Deas worked with the Blind, he does not seem to have placed the same emphasis on general work with schools and indeed appears to have rejected the idea of a schools loan service when it was put forward by William Smallcombe. The lack of development of school services in Sunderland was hindered by inter

An early example of interactive exhibits: children handling archaeological objects in the 1970s.

departmental tension between the Education department and the Libraries & Museums department.

A programme of work with schools started in October 1939, just after James Crawley had become Director. Nevin Drinkwater, the Deputy Curator, spoke to three classes of children each week on subjects such as prehistoric man, mammals, the aquaria, pottery and local geology. These classes continued until the late 1950s.

Until the 1970s the Museum did not have any formal education service but provided help to teachers and lecturers at the Teacher Training College through an informal loans service, and in other ways.

In the 1960s the museum became a base for further education in Sunderland. Both Durham University Extra-mural and Workers Associations classes were held in the museum, sometimes they were led by museum staff and sometimes by lecturers from outside. One of these was David Bellamy of Durham University who went on to achieve international fame.

Museum staff also played a part in local societies such as the Sunderland Antiquarian Society, Sunderland Natural History Society, Natural History Society of Northumbria and the Durham County Conservation Trust. Several groups including the Antiquarians, Natural History Society, Pianoforte Society, Gramophone Music Society and the Sunderland Art Gallery Concert Society (following concerts in the Second World War organised by the Council for the Encouragement of Music and the Arts) have held their meetings at the Museum.

When Tyne and Wear Museums was established in 1975 education officers were appointed. They were initially based in Newcastle but activities were also arranged in Sunderland, and the Tyne & Wear Young Naturalists Club - organised in conjunction with the natural sciences staff - was started. It still operates successfully today.

In 1982, the first education officer was appointed at Sunderland Museum and started a loans service, teachers packs, teachers meetings, sessions for B.Ed. students and schools. Workshops for chools involving local artists and craft people, and object-based sessions led by the Museum's educational staff, were also developed during the 1980s and 1990s. Classes for adults were also started including art, calligraphy, craft subjects and local history. The classes have produced work for display in the Museum, such as the Museum Alphabet and the Museum Quilt.

Services to visitors to the museum have been equally important, and have included quizsheets for children, and family activities during holidays. Community-based projects, involving both adults and children, during holiday periods have produced such work as the lifeboat hooky mat, the Staithes Group Wallhanging and the Tiger Rug.

Working with groups with disabilities has been another important feature of the museum in recent years, as with Charlton Deas's activities at the turn of the Century. Working with groups of people with all types of disabilities is a regular feature of exhibitions and has gained the Museum several awards.

Charlton Deas's work with people with disabilities

Charlton Deas was a pioneer in making museums available to people with disabilities, especially blind children. He organised seven sessions in 1913 for blind adults and their friends on successive Sunday afternoons, followed by a session on Monday morning for blind children.

It may seem unusual to demonstrate paintings to blind people, but Charlton Deas did this successfully. "First, a short explanation of the purpose of pictures was given; then, a small painted and unpainted canvas, an artist's palette, brushes, and paint tubes were handed to each individual to feel

A DOZEN DON'TS IN DEALING WITH THE BLIND.

By J. A. CHARLTON DEAS, M.A.,

Director of the Sunderland Public Libraries, Museum and Art Gallery.

1. DON'T treat the blind as though they were abnormal specimens of humanity. Never talk to a blind man as though he were deaf, or imagine that the mere possession of sight implies superior knowledge.

2. DON'T refer to blindness as an "affliction"; it is a "handicap." Never express sympathy for a blind person in his hearing, for you don't please him any more than you would a cripple by discussing lameness in his presence; there are more practical outlets.

3. DON'T try to carry a blind person when he is entering a tram or train, crossing a road, or going upstairs. He is not usually lame, and only needs to have his hand placed on a handle or rail. A touch on the arm is sufficient for leading. You need not help him to sit down once he knows the position of his chair.

4. DON'T "tack" when piloting him across a road, go straight across if possible; otherwise you may upset his reckoning or cause him to side-stumble on reaching the kerb. Sound and touch are the blind man's "sight," so do not push him before you in strange places, in order to see where he is going; go first, his hand touching you, that he may "see" where you are going.

5. DON'T think that a blind guest is a serious responsibility, will break up your home, or need someone to dress, bib and feed him! To leave him a candle, and locate the looking-glass, are not infrequent errors.

6. DON'T address a blind man through an intermediary. For instance, don't ascertain if he takes sugar to tea, by enquiring of his wife or friend; his own mentality is usually capable of enlightening you on any such matter.

7. DON'T make unusual revisions in conversation, such as withdrawing the word "see," and substituting "heard." Use the word "blind" without hesitation, if you are discussing "blindness" with those so handicapped, but don't substitute this topic for the weather.

8. DON'T fail to speak, if only a word, on entering a room in which there is a blind person; it announces your presence, and helps identification. Say who you are, if a stranger. Always shake hands when meeting or leaving a blind friend; for a handshake is as expressive as the face, and is the substitute for the smile of friendship.

9. DON'T take it for granted that every blind person is a musician—or an idiot! Refrain from continually exclaiming "wonderful" or "marvellous" because he can do quite usual things, such as—tell the time by his watch, fill and light his pipe, or discover that it has gone out.

10. DON'T talk of an "extra sense," or "providential compensations," and so perpetuate an obstinate delusion. The so-called "miraculous" is only extra development.

11. DON'T limit your knowledge and interest in the blind generally, to the street mendicant, who is frequently a social parasite from choice.

12. DON'T be patronising with the blind, always be natural, and never fail in real kindness, for—"you never know, you know!"

and examine closely. After a description of the nature and use of these materials, the blind visitors were taken to the pictures, glazed ones being selected for obvious reasons. Their length and height, and the character of the frames were felt with considerable interest, the great size of many being a revelation which drew forth expressions of surprise. After the subject of a picture had been described, the positions of the important features were indicated by guiding the first finger of the person's hands over the outlines, and in this way their relative location and size of the principal points were made clear".

On the next three Sundays there were sessions on natural history, followed by human anatomy and miscellaneous objects.

As well as a lecture, there was a handling session in which specimens of different animals were taken out of their cases and the blind visitors encouraged to feel them. This way, the blind people could experience Lions, a Polar Bear, Eagle, Shark, Crocodile, human skeleton, Zulu shields and spears and even the parrot that used to live in the Winter Gardens.

Activities like this are now a normal part of the work of a museum's education section, but in 1913 they were innovative. The reaction of the blind children is somewhat telling: they were astounded with the way they were treated by the museum because, as one commented "We are mainly accustomed to be treated as if we were something less than human beings".

One of the guided walks organised by the Museum each summer. This group, on the Victoria Bridge in June 1988 for the 150th anniversary of its opening, included British Rail safety staff.

Councillor Ralph Baxter (left), Vice-Chairman of Tyne and Wear Joint Museums Committee, Robert Key M.P. (centre), Under Secretary of State at the Department of National Heritage and Neil Sinclair (right), Senior Curator, at the presentation of the B.T. North East Museum and Gallery Customer Care award in 1992.

Awards

In 1974 Monkwearmouth Station Museum received a special runners-up award in the *Museum of the Year* competition, a major achievement for a small museum as the major award that year was won by the National Motor Museum. Since 1991 Tyne and Wear Museums has won more awards than any other museum service in the country, and Sunderland Museum and Art Gallery has won the greatest number of awards within Tyne and Wear. They are:

1991 National Heritage Museum of the Year Award. Winner: Best Museum Education Initiative.

1992 B.T. North East Museum and Gallery Awards. Winner: Customer Care.

1992 Sunderland Echo Quill Award

1993 Gulbenkian Awards. Highly commended: Best Provision for Visitors with Disabilities.

1993 B.T. North East Museum and Gallery Awards. Winner: Best Community Initiative (for *B.P. Re-vision*)

1994 National Art Collections Fund Awards. Winner: *Sunderland's Glorious Glass*, plus Highly Commended: Education Programme.

1994 Interpret Britain Awards. Commendation: *...And Ships Were Born*

1994 B.T. North East Museums and Gallery Awards. Runner-up: Favourite Children's Visit (Monkwearmouth Station Museum). Runner-up: Provision for People with Disabilities (Monkwearmouth Station Museum).

1995 Interpret Britain Awards. Commendation: *Sunderland's Glorious Glass*.

Staff in Jan. 1932 BACK ROW(left to right) Attendants: Eltringham (Central Reading Rooms); King (Art Gallery); ?; Atkinson (Art Gallery); Francis (Chief Janitor); Sergeant (Art Gallery); McVey (Central Reading Rooms); Brown (West Branch); Moir (Reading Rooms). SECOND ROW (left to right): Mrs McNicol (retired); Mrs Taylor (Art Gallery attendant); Mrs Cousins (Art Gallery Attendant); ?; Nancy Davidson (Library Assistant); Vera Lawrence (Library Assistant); Kathleen Mair (Library Assistant); Mrs Atkinson (part-time Art Gallery Attendant); Doris Brown (Bindery). MIDDLE ROW (left to right), all Library staff: Isabella Scott; Edith Koerber; Elsie Cowens; Kathleen Tansey; Nora Cunningham; Mary Bell; Mary Wright; Holmes; Constance Chapman; Margaret Turner. FRONT ROW (left to right): Margaret Kennedy (Branch Librarian Monkwearmouth); Catherine Ellis (Branch Librarian West); Marie Louise Coatsworth (Senior Woman Librarian); Bob Lyde (Senior Assistant Librarian, later Deputy); James Crawley (Deputy Director, later Director); J.A. Charlton Deas (Director); George Nevin Drinkwater (Deputy Curator); James A. Burnett (Senior Assistant Librarian); Rachel Woodman (Branch Librarian, Hendon); Gatenby (Branch Librarian, Southwick). SEATED: left, Tom Shaw (Library Assistant, later Director); right, Willis (Museum Youth). (Thanks to Tom Shaw, for being able to put names to all but two of these faces after an interval of sixty four years).

Sunderland Museums staff in 1996 BACK ROW (left to right): Gordon Charlton; Alan Burnett; Peter Gibson; John Hayes; Fred Hagel; Bob Weldon; George Norton; George Patterson; Jim Gray. STANDING (left to right): Alf Duncan; Jim Midwood; Alison Ross; Barbara Collar; Helen Fothergill; Lorna Storey; Maureen Farrow; Margaret Lancaster; Barbara Johnson; Kath Fenwick; Les Jessop; Betty Watson; Martin Routledge; Tony Drake. SEATED (left to right): Emma Willson; Jo Cunningham; Helen Sinclair; Neil Sinclair; Juliet Horsley; Sue Newell; Judy Sunley.

EIGHT

RUNNING A MUSEUM

How is the museum funded?

The National Museums obtain most of their funding from Central Government, and most local authority museums are funded through the local council. Councils can no longer raise money on the rates directly to pay for their museums, and the funds come from part of the total budget of the local authority.

Tyne and Wear Museums is a complex organisation compared with most other local authority museums, and there is a special arrangement for funding it. As long as the five districts continue to run the service jointly the government provides, *via* the Museums and Galleries Commission, a considerable amount of money towards its costs in addition to the money provided by the councils.

As well as money from local and national government, money must be raised from outside bodies if we are to continue to put on new exhibitions and displays. This comes either in the form of sponsorship from businesses, money from charities, or special funds like the Heritage Lottery Fund. Significant sums are given in grants from the North of England Museums Service.

Chairmen and Committees

Like all organisations in local government, a committee of councillors is ultimately responsible, and democratically accountable, for the Tyne & Wear Museums.

There has been a committee of councillors responsible for running the Museum since Sunderland Corporation took it over in 1846. The *Tyne & Wear Joint Museums Committee* now in charge of Tyne and Wear Museums has members drawn from Gateshead (4), Newcastle (6), South Tyneside (4), North Tyneside (4) and Sunderland (5)

The periods of greatest development in the Museum have often been when there has

been an influential Chairman and supportive committee.

The Committees have had several long-serving councillors, notably Robert Cameron in the 1870s-90s, and J.S. Nicholson in the inter-war years. More recently Ralph Baxter has been Vice- Chairman of the Tyne and Wear Joint Museums Committee since its formation in 1986.

Before 1974 the committee also had co-opted members. In the 20th Century these included the Director of Education, and the Principals of the Technical College and College of Art. Richard Ray, Principal of the Art College, continued as a co-opted member after he retired and served on the committee for over 40 years. In 1934 other co-opted members included J. Hall and T.R. Milburn, both noted architects, J.W. Corder, the local historian, and Sir Luke Thompson, one of Sunderland's M.Ps.

Attendant staff are much more than just guardians of the galleries: they are the public faces of the Museum and are responsible for customer care.

Staffing

Attendants

Many people use the term 'Museum Curator' to refer to the attendants - the people in uniform you see in the galleries. A letter in the *Sunday Sun* in 1995 lamented the number of qualifications needed to get a job these days, saying that if it gets any worse "even museum curators will need degrees".

The museums in Sunderland currently employ 13 attendants. Both the Borough Road building and Monkwearmouth Station Museum have a Senior Attendant and a Chief Attendant. The attendants are the public face of the museum, providing customer care: they are the first port of call for enquiries, they control security, liaise with contractors about building work, operate the shop and on many occasions help to install exhibitions: and one of the attendants does actually have a University degree!

Sunderland Museum is known to have employed an attendant when it was housed in the Athenaeum. When the Borough Road building was opened in 1879 the Curator James Bowley appears to have assumed the role of attendant in ensuring security for the museum.

In August 1905 G. Stacey, who had been a Sergeant Major with the Royal Artillery Garrison at Sunderland Barracks, was appointed caretaker at a salary of £1.00 per week plus free housing, gas and uniform. The janitor's flat at that time was on the 3rd floor of the building below the dome: a new flat was provided in the 1960s extension until 1981.

From 1915 preference was given to men who had served in the armed forces when attendants were being appointed, and many from then until the 1980s had a military background. One of the best remembered of these was Charles West, Chief Janitor from 1932-1956, who was said to carry out his work "with military precision".

Curators and other staff

As for the curators, the *Sunday Sun* reader might be surprised to learn that they all have degrees! There are specialists in Natural History, Art, Education, History, Science and Archaeology, who divide their time between the different museums in Tyne and Wear. Tyne and Wear Museums also employs administrative, marketing, design, commercial, conservation and technical staff.

There may have been honorary curators in the period of the Subscription Museum, but their names are not known. The earliest curator we are aware of is William King, who was appointed in 1837. In the early years, the curator of the museum was not a full-time position. In 1865, James W. Kirkby was appointed as curator at a salary of £25 a year, but he only worked 48 days at eight hours per day (presumably, one day a week with four 'weeks' holiday). In the same year the previous curator, Dr Evans, was asked to return some books belonging to the museum and claimed in return that he was owed £60 arrears in salary - more than two years' pay!

Later, the post of curator became a full-time occupation. Until 1905 the man in charge of the museum was known as the *Curator*. When Charlton Deas was appointed as head of both the library and the museum in 1905 he was called the *Director*, and below him was a curator responsible for the museum. Over the subsequent years this deputy's post has had a variety of titles, including Deputy Curator, Senior Curator, and Principal Assistant Curator.

After the Second World War the museum profession criticised the practice of combining Librarian's and Curator's jobs, but in Sunderland the system worked well. This was shown by the town contributing the best-run museums to the new Tyne and Wear Museums Service in 1974.

The combination of the Library and the Museum was successful largely because both operated as equal and complementary partners. This was probably due to Shaw and Kirtley's experience in both fields. It was also because of the degree of autonomy given to Jim Wilson, Principal Assistant Curator, and the other museum staff. Several of the staff during this period went on to occupy influential positions in the museum world elsewhere.

With the creation of Tyne & Wear County and the county-wide museums service in 1974, the administration of the library and museum in Sunderland was separated and the Librarians and Curators no longer report to the same Director. The current *Director of Tyne & Wear Museums* is in charge of all of the council-run museums and art galleries in the county, and there is a *Senior Curator* who is responsible for the Sunderland Museums.

Curators to 1905

1837 - 1840	Professor William King
1840 - 1865	Dr John Evans
1865 - 1866	James Walker Kirkby
1866 - 1868	George Clifton Pecket
1868 - 1913	Robert Cameron J.P., M.P. (honorary curator)
1895 - 1905	Captain James M.E. Bowley

Directors of Sunderland Library, Museum and Art Gallery

1905 - 1939	J.A. Charlton Deas
1939 - 1960	James Crawley
1960 - 1973	J. Thomas Shaw
1973 - 1974	Ernest Kirtley

Directors of Tyne and Wear Museums

1974 - 1975	Kenneth Barton
1975 - 1991	John Thompson
1991 -	Dr David Fleming

Curators since 1905

1905 - 1912	Gilbert Henry Dutton
1912 - 1921	Herbert M. Ricketts
1921 - 1922	T. Russell Goddard
1922 - 1926	William Smallcombe
1926 - 1929	Norman Sylvester
1929 - 1947	George Nevin Drinkwater
1947 - 1977	James H. Wilson
1977 -	Neil T. Sinclair

Several of the staff at Sunderland have gone on to become curators or directors of other museums. The Hancock Museum has had no fewer than three curators who previously worked at Sunderland (William King, Russell Goddard and Alec Coles).

Other museums and art galleries whose heads have previously worked at Sunderland include; the Shipley Art Gallery (Nevin Drinkwater and Marilyn Carr), Halifax Museums (Ronald Innes and Rosie Crook), Derby (Gilbert Dutton), Reading (William Smallcombe), Darlington (Alan Suddes), Doncaster and Bournemouth (Norman Sylvester), Ironbridge Gorge Museum (Stuart Smith), Stockport (John Baker), Portsmouth (Charles Steel), Exeter and Bristol (Hilary McGowan), and Monmouth, Ipswich and Coventry (Alf Hatton).

Daniel Herdman became Librarian and Curator at Cheltenham and was also Honorary Secretary of the Museums Association in 1929 and 1957

Warner Haldane went to New Zealand, where he became curator first of Gisborne then Whakatane Museums

Other staff have gone on to occupy influential positions in training. Geoff Stansfield became a lecturer on the very first Museums Studies course in Britain at Leicester University in 1966, and Alf Hatton went on to the Museums Studies course at the Institute of Archaeology and at the Ironbridge Gorge Institute. More recently, Peter Davis started a Museums Studies course at Newcastle University in 1992. In a slightly different field, Jim Devenport was appointed lecturer on the first Art Conservation course run successively by Gateshead Technical College and the University of Northumbria.

Professor William King

Professor King was a local man, born in Low Row, Bishopwearmouth in 1808: his father was a "coal caster" (whose job was loading and trimming coals on collier vessels) and his mother kept a confectioner's shop. In 1833 William King opened a bookshop and stationery shop at 205 High Street West, and this became a meeting place for the Sunderland *literati*. He was secretary and librarian to the Sunderland Literary and Philosophical Society, and between 1837 and 1840 he was the first Curator of the Sunderland Museum.

King had a keen interest in geology from his schooldays onwards, and appears to have supplemented his income by dealing in fossils and minerals. In 1840, he was appointed as Curator of the Newcastle Museum, in terms of status definitely a step up from his work at Sunderland but the move cost him money and he was allowed to supplement his salary by continuing his rock-dealing business.

There was a serious quarrel between King and other geologists in Newcastle, which resulted in him leaving in 1848 and eventually moving to Queen's College, Galway. His major work, *A Monograph of the Permian Fossils of England* was published in 1850.

From humble beginnings William King ended his career as Professor of Natural History, an honorary Doctor of Science and with an eventual entry in the *Dictionary of National Biography.*

James Walker Kirkby, Curator 1865-1866.

James Walker Kirkby

J. W. Kirkby was the second and last of the 'geological' curators in charge of Sunderland Museum. Born at Bishopwearmouth on April 10th 1834, Kirkby was a cousin of the Hancock brothers of Newcastle. Educated at a private school on Bishopwearmouth Green, Kirkby seems to have become interested in geology as a child.

Although he had a long and serious interest in geology and an international reputation as an expert in his field, Kirkby did not follow William King into an academic career. Rather, he was by profession a colliery manager. Kirkby trained locally at Etherley Colliery and later (in 1867) moved to Fife where he was manager of Pirnie Colliery. His spell as curator of Sunderland Museum can only be regarded as an aside to his mining career. In later years, Kirkby donated a large collection of fossils to the Hancock Museum in Newcastle, probably because of his family connections.

Robert Cameron M.P. was Chairman of the Museum and Art Gallery Committee and Honorary Curator of the Museum for many years.

Robert Cameron

Robert Cameron (1825-1913) was a major figure in education and local government at the end of the 19th century in Sunderland, and influential in furthering the cause of the Museum.

Cameron was born in Perthshire, the son of a Baptist Minister, and was a Gaelic speaker who only learned English when he was 18. He must have mastered the language quickly because after he had been to training college in London, in 1866 he became Headmaster of the British School in Norfolk Street (the building still survives as part of the Norfolk Hotel). He remained Headmaster of the British School for 47 years.

When the Sunderland School Board was established in 1871 Cameron became a member and was its Chairman from 1877 to 1885. He was also town councillor from 1876 to 1892 and an Alderman from 1892 to 1896. Cameron retired from the town council a year after he had been elected as Liberal MP for Houghton-le-Spring, a seat which he held until his death in 1913.

Cameron was a pioneer of further education, organising science and literary classes. In the winter of 1874-75, for instance, he delivered nine scientific lectures at Easington Lane. He was also a JP, a founder of the Sunderland YMCA, a campaigner in support of prohibition of alcohol, and a lay preacher both in Congregational and Primitive Methodist churches. At the age of 72 when he was an MP he was preaching every weekend at chapels throughout England.

With the other roles he played in public life in Sunderland, it is not surprising that Robert Cameron was a major influence in the development of Sunderland Museum. He was initially a co-opted member of the Libraries & Museums Committee, and in 1868 became the Honorary Curator following the resignation of G.C. Pecket. He remained as Honorary Curator until his death in 1913 although he appears to have had little active involvement after becoming an MP in 1895. He was also Chairman of the Libraries & Museums Committee for 10 years.

It seems certain that Robert Cameron was a major force in encouraging Sunderland Corporation to build the Museum & Library. Cameron himself took the lead in arranging the exhibits and he was similarly closely involved with the opening of the Art Gallery in 1880.

His obituary in the *Museums Journal* stated that at Sunderland: "he built up a collection there that for orderly arrangement, educational effectiveness and popular charm was rarely excelled".

James Bowley

James Bowley, a Naval Chief Petty Officer, was appointed to the Museum staff under the Honorary Curator John Cameron in 1879 when the new building opened. He appears to have been involved in both attendant and curatorial duties. In 1895 when Cameron became an MP Bowley was appointed Curator.

As Curator, Bowley had an assistant and an attendant, responsible for admission to the Art Gallery, to assist him. He himself, however, still seems to have been responsible for the security of the museum. In December 1898 he was reported in the *Sunderland Daily Echo* as saying:

" .. if the Committee could see their way to appoint a man to watch the Museum, it would give him more time to perform the duties of a Curator, and he could proceed much quicker with the naming of the objects."

His plea was unsuccessful and when he retired in 1905 it was recorded that:

"he with naval step has patrolled many thousands of miles up and down the entrance hall".

On his retirement in 1905 Bowley lamented the fact that literally hundreds of Museum treasures were stored away, and he hoped that the Corporation would proceed with a proposed new building between the Museum & Library and the Palatine Hotel. The collections had certainly grown during Bowley's curatorship and he was responsible for mounting the first display of Sunderland pottery in 1900.

J.A. Charlton Deas, Director 1905-1939

J.A. Charlton Deas

J.A. Charlton Deas (1874-1951) has become a legendary figure in Sunderland. If he was delayed in leaving the Museum the Chief Attendant would be sent with orders "hold the London train for Mr. Deas". He once reported a Police Sergeant for not saluting him when he was leaving the Museum.

Deas also had a reputation throughout the museum world as a stern disciplinarian. Tom Shaw who worked as the Museum Assistant in the 1930s recalls dropping a mediaeval pot in the entrance hall when mounting a display. Deas shot out of his adjacent office and instantly dismissed him, although fortunately he later relented and Tom Shaw went on to become Director. An example of the hierarchy of the office in his time is that the telephone system allowed Deas to phone other staff, but they could not phone him!

The colourful side of Charlton Deas should not, however, obscure his importance as an innovator in the museum world during the 1900s and 1910s. He was a pioneer in circulating temporary exhibitions, working with blind people and in publicising museums.

Charlton Deas trained as a librarian in Newcastle and was appointed Chief Librarian in Sunderland in 1904. When James Bowley retired in 1905 Deas was appointed as Director of Libraries & Museums although not without opposition; his appointment was approved by the Council on an 18 to 14 vote.

Deas was responsible for several developments in the Library, including the introduction of an open-access system and construction of three branch libraries financed by Andrew Carnegie. He introduced major changes to the Museum including abolishing the admission charge to the Art Gallery in 1906. He also started a regular series of temporary exhibitions and was an advocate of travelling art exhibitions which could circulate round the country. In 1911 he spoke to the Museums Association conference in Brighton advocating circulating major loans from national collections. This has only really been achieved in the 1990s when Sunderland has received 'masterpiece' loans from both the Tate and National Galleries.

In 1913 Charlton Deas was again addressing the Museums Association conference, this time about 'The showing of Museums and Art Galleries to the Blind' based on his experience in Sunderland. King George V and Queen Mary expressed an interest in reports of his work with blind people: When they visited Durham and Lambton Castle later in 1913 some of the models made by blind children at the Museum were sent for their inspection. In 1927 Deas, as President of the Museums Association, met the King and Queen at the opening of the new National Museum of Wales and they evidently recalled his involvement with blind people.

In contrast to Charlton Deas's role in developing the museum's services, the collections grew slowly during his Directorship and the Museum Room developed little. This was partly a reflection of his plans for a new extension: he felt that there was not much point in collecting further exhibits until the extension to the Museum & Library had been completed. In 1938 the Corporation agreed to the scheme at a cost of £50,000 (£41,000 for the Museum & Library extension and £9,000 for a new Winter Gardens at the south of the lake). In July 1939, a few months after the proposal of the scheme, Charlton Deas retired. He reflected that the extension scheme for the Museum & Library was still in the air, but it had been in the air when he had arrived in 1905. The outbreak of war killed any hope of providing more space for the Museum & Library.

An indication of his training as a Librarian was shown when he stated in his Presidential address to the Museums Association that there was, "the need in many public galleries for periodical weeding. Discarding out-of-date pictures is as important as discarding out-of-date books. ... no good purpose is served by retaining pictures which have long since had their day and been surpassed by better work".

He had forceful views on art. In 1938, for instance, he denounced surrealism as 'Bolshevism in Art'.

From 1905, staff involved in the Museum were the Director, Deputy Director, Deputy Curator, and an Assistant who was a male school leaver (the library assistants were female), and at least one Attendant. The Deputy Director was a librarian but also had some involvement in the Museum. From 1905 to 1922 the post was held by Daniel Herdman who went on to be librarian-curator at Cheltenham, and from 1926 to 1939 by James Crawley, who was eventually to succeed Deas as Director.

There were five Deputy Curators between 1905 and 1929, the number probably reflected personality clashes between Deas and some of his staff. The longest period of stability was achieved in 1929 when George Nevin Drinkwater, from the teaching museum at the Royal Dental Hospital, was appointed Deputy Curator and stayed for 17 years.

George Nevin Drinkwater, Deputy Curator 1929-1947.

Drinkwater had a particular interest in fine art, and developed the records for this collection. He evidently wrote sermons for the Liberal Catholic Church in Newcastle, where he was priest-in-charge during his time at the museum. When Charlton Deas arrived in his office he would lean forward to push his writing ledge with his sermon back into his desk! In 1946 Drinkwater became Curator of the Shipley Art Gallery in Gateshead and built up a picture conservation studio and a full-time course in picture restoration which is now run by the University of Northumbria.

James Crawley, Tom Shaw and Ernest Kirtley

J.A. Charlton Deas was Director of Sunderland Libraries and Museum & Art Gallery for 34 years, up to 1939. There were three further holders of the post before it disappeared in local authority reorganisation in 1974 - James Crawley, Tom Shaw and Ernest Kirtley. During their period in charge of the Museum it developed greatly in size, staffing and collections.

James Crawley, Director 1939-1960.

James Crawley worked in Newcastle Library and had been Deputy Director under Deas for ten years before succeeding him. He saw the Museum through the difficult wartime years before the expansion of the Museum service began again in 1955 with the opening of Grindon Museum and the major extension completed in 1964.

Tom Shaw, Director 1960-1973.

James Crawley retired just after the foundation stone of the extension had been laid in 1960. He was succeeded by Tom Shaw who worked in the Museum and Library for forty four years. He joined the Museum in 1929 when he answered the following advertisement in the *Sunderland Echo*:

"**YOUTH WANTED** for Sunderland Public Museum; must show evidence of special interest in Natural History, and possess the University of Durham School Certificate."

Applicants had to apply in person to the Deputy Curator of the Museum. Tom Shaw recalled that:

"I seemed to spend the first three years painting the insides of the cases in the natural history section, and cleaning up the stuffed birds and varnishing their legs and beaks"

After three years Tom Shaw moved to the Library where he felt there were more career opportunities. He was succeeded as the 'museum youth' by Ernest Kirtley, who also later moved to be a librarian. Both joined the Sunderland-based 125th Anti-Tank Regiment, R.A.; during World War II Tom Shaw was transferred to another regiment while Ernest Kirtley was one of the members of the 125th who was captured at Singapore by the Japanese.

Tom Shaw became Deputy Director of the Museum in 1948 and was Director from 1960 to 1973. Ernest Kirtley again followed him in both posts and was the last Director of the Libraries, Museum and Art Gallery in Sunderland before the department was broken up in 1974. Their years as Director were marked by major expansion of the museum service at Sunderland and Monkwearmouth Station Museums.

James Wilson

James Wilson began his museum career at Salford Royal Museum and Art Gallery and came to Sunderland in 1947 to be interviewed for the post of Senior Assistant Curator. He was initially horrified by the old-fashioned nature of the Museum recalling that

"I took one look at the place and my first thought was to get the next train back to Manchester"

However, he decided to accept the job, partly because of the friendly nature of the staff. Tom Shaw and Ernest Kirtley offered him a cigarette (then in short supply) and took him for a tram ride to Seaburn which was bathed in glorious sunshine.

Jim Wilson was a multi-talented curator during a period when subject specialisation was rare in all but the largest local authority museums. He became an expert on Sunderland's local history, artists, glass and pottery, and wrote the first edition of *The Potteries of Sunderland and District* in 1951. He combined this with the practical work, planning and mounting displays, and framing paintings.

His memories included receiving a donation 'which had been found among a cargo of scrap iron at South Dock': "I arrived at work one day to find a five foot box on my desk. Hearing weird noises coming from inside it, I opened it up and there was a five-foot long Iguana looking very angry about the whole situation". The PDSA were contacted and the Iguana became the centre of attention at their stand at the Seaburn Show before they found it a suitable home.

Jim Wilson has continued his interest in the Museum since retirement. In 1994 he was

Jim Wilson and Jim Devenport preparing an exhibition of glassware.

presented with Life Membership of the Museums Association to mark the fact that he had been a member for 60 years.

Annie McNicol

In the early days of the Borough Road Museum, a female attendant took umbrellas and walking sticks from visitors to the art gallery on the first floor, and was responsible for taking the fees charged for these.

In 1885 Mrs Annie McNicol was appointed to the post and she did not retire until 1929, after 34 years full-time and 10 years part-time service. After retiring, Mrs McNicol lived in the Almshouses beside Bishopwearmouth Church, but still returned every few months to do some dusting, for which she was paid 2/6 from petty cash: a way of giving some extra income to add to her pension. Her obituary in November 1936 recorded that she had "an attractive and cheerful personality, and had an intimate acquaintance with old Sunderland".

NINE

OPINIONS AND MEMOIRS, THEN & NOW

1893: Robert Blair's review

[Robert Blair published this review of Sunderland Museum in *The Antiquary* in 1893. Obviously, his opinions of the value of the displays were mixed!]

The Free Library and Museum building is a fine structure of stone, in what, I suppose, is called French Renaissance style, erected a few years ago in Borough Road, which it faces, its back being towards the park. Its dimensions are about 210 feet long by 60 feet wide, and is much too small for so large a town as Sunderland, with a populace of considerably about 150,000 souls. The building is divided into two equal parts by a vestibule in the centre, about 30 feet wide. This is approached from the street by a flight of stone steps, while on the opposite side - the south - there is a door, which is seldom or ever open, leading into a conservatory, which extends the whole length of the building. To this conservatory there is access from the park. In the vestibule models of steamships which have in recent years been built on the Wear are exhibited; and the room is further adorned by statues and busts of local men of note.

The long room on the right hand (which is a little smaller than that on the left, as a staircase is taken off it) is divided into two storeys, the lower room being the library, and the upper a picture-gallery. In many

The Antiquities Room in December 1960. Most of the floor of this room was removed to enlarge the Entrance Hall area in the development scheme, but the far end remains as the Tea Room.

towns much smaller than Sunderland, the circulating and reference departments of the library, and the newspapers, are all in different rooms, while here all are cramped into the one room, a state of things not to be commended. The library, moreover, judging from appearances, which perhaps is not always a safe mode of judging, is very poor, and not only so, but the books have a grimy, dingy look, utterly beneath the dignity of the town. I have been told that there is a small ladies' room off the main library, but it is said to be 'disgusting' - the word used by a lady when describing it to me. The upper storey, as I have already said, contains a small collection of oil-paintings, none of any note. But whether of note or otherwise, every picture should have a descriptive label attached to it, instead of visitors being compelled to purchase a catalogue.

The natural history collection is housed in the opposite - the left - wing, and the full height of the building is utilised for the purpose, the upper portion of the room being surrounded by wide galleries. This collection is all that could be desired, I think, well-kept and cared for, with no lack of labels. The only objects of antiquarian interest, however, in it are the mummified body of a woman from the guano beds of Peru, and a collection of skulls and other bones, including human, in cases in the gallery at the West end. Some of these remains are from the neighbourhood of Sunderland, such as those of prehistoric date from a cave at Ryhope, and those dredged from the river Wear at Claxheugh. As giving a clue to the age of the last named, it may be stated that a fine bronze rapier blade of Ancient British manufacture, was a short time ago dug out of the sand by the side of the river at Claxheugh. This has been added to the valuable collection of Canon Greenwell. To come at last to the special object of this paper, the antiquarian collection, which is shown in the badly-smelling, ill-ventilated

The Museum in 1992, with banners celebrating the granting of 'City' status to Sunderland.

room above the vestibule - ill-ventilated is not the word, seeing that there is an utter absence of all ventilation not only here but throughout the building. It is approached, as is also the picture-gallery, by the staircase before mentioned.

There is also a way into this room from the gallery of the natural history, but the door has always been locked when I have visited the museum; if this door were occasionally, though I do not see why it should not always be, open, the stagnant air in the room would be set in motion and driven out. The objects are displayed in glazed cases, chiefly against the wall.

[there then follows a list of objects in the antiquities gallery]

Perhaps a few words may be permitted. The chief object of those in charge of the establishment seems to be to make as much as possible out of the picture-gallery and antiquarian portion, and this in a paltry way, too, notwithstanding the fact that the museum is supported out of the rates. A charge of one penny per head, not a large sum, certainly, is levied for admission to the portions in question every day in the week, except Thursday, one penny being demanded for taking care of a stick or umbrella, while the natural history portion is open every day free, and no one is as much as asked for his stick or umbrella. Why there should be this distinction it puzzles a stranger to make out, seeing that many of the objects in the natural history museum, such as butterflies, shells, etc., are much more fragile, and therefore more liable to injury than the more substantial objects in the antiquarian room, like stone axes, earthenware pots, etc.

In conclusion, it may be stated in justice to the memory of my friend, the late Captain T.W.U. Robinson, F.S.A., of Houghton-le-Spring, that but for his extensive and valuable gifts of antiquities to the museum shortly before his death, it would not have been necessary for me to have written this description, as, so far as antiquities are

(*Sunderland Echo*, February 18, 1929)

Wild Snowballing in Mowbray Park

Flower Beds Trampled On During Disgraceful Scenes

POLICE TURN OUT CROWD

Wintry Weather, "With Some Snow", Expected to Continue

Cold weather and bright sunshine attracted a crowd of 10,000 to Mowbray Park, and friendly snowballing rapidly got out of hand. Park staff retreated under a barrage of snowballs, and even women with prams were hit as hundreds of youngsters went wild. At 4 p.m. the police were called in to clear the park, and as youths were ushered away museum attendants regulating the queues for the museum became the target for snowballs.

Some of the crowd then moved into the building, as it was reported "The museum was closed early because of the risk of damage to exhibits by the noisy crowd, who packed the precincts of the buildings".

The Director said "When Sunday opening was introduced nine years ago, the average attendance was 280 - almost entirely of the class of person for whom the facilities were intended. For some time now however, a section of youths have used the place as a covered promenade rather than for purposes of instruction and the attendants have continually to move on groups who persist in chattering. There is a tendency to shuffle aimlessly round the building in a drove from one room to another to the annoyance of the 25% of people who are actually interested in the exhibits".

concerned, there would have been very few, if any, to describe.

1910s: Memoirs by L.G. Grimshaw

The Sunderland museum in the north end of Mowbray Park was a good one. When I returned and went through it in 1960 it appeared completely unchanged. I could recognise everything that I had seen when I was young. On one side downstairs was a conservatory filled with plants and tropical birds, and on the other side were beautifully made models of ships and locomotives......It was among these models, when I was a small boy, that I was hesitantly approached by two poor women and asked to read to them some of the descriptive signs; the poor women were illiterate, and would have been ashamed to ask an adult to read for them.

You walk up to the second floor of the museum passing a magnificent male walrus on the landing. Upstairs are the stuffed animals and birds; the male lion is one that died in a travelling show years ago, and is considered to be one of the largest lions known. In cases, shielded from the light, are collections of butterflies and beetles. I used to collect beetles, as I have said, and was naturally interested in them.....

About 1914-1919: memories of the Art Gallery

By S.M. Stacey, who, as the head Janitor's son at that time, lived in a flat in the building.

The wall colour was a greyish green, but this of course could well have been a light olive green. The walls were so crowded with pictures, that no one ever noticed the colour of the walls. The pictures were hung very "higgledy piggledy", the larger at the base and the other smaller ones placed anywhere they would fit! Very close together, like the effect shown in pictures of old Victorian drawing rooms. I well remember having to crane my head upwards to read the caption on the picture of the "High Priest" in order to ascertain the jewels on his breast-plate!

Lord Leighton's statue of "An athlete struggling with a python" was centrally

placed - a horrible Plasticine blue colour - and was surrounded at the base by four beautiful large green jardiniäres, complete with small palms. I painfully remember these as I was most unfortunate in breaking one! The floor was of light brown, best quality linoleum up to within about 30 inches of the walls. The remaining surround was stained deep brown, and the surbase black. The lino was handwashed twice a month by charwomen and oiled on Sundays by a dreadful thing called "Oleo Dust Allayer". The stanchions [rope-barrier supports] were about 6' apart brass topped and connected to each other by deep red cordage, also brass ended. Swing screens were used for print exhibitions, but because they were accident prone were replaced by 4 standard green baize covered screens.

The roof was painted cream, and on the "sunny" side of the gallery, hand operated curtains were fitted to the skylights, also cream, as a protection to the pictures.

1964: childhood visits

By Les. Jessop, later to become Keeper of Biology.

It must have been in my last year at junior school that I used to come into the museum on a Saturday with my friends. The smell of polish gave the place a distinctive odour that I instantly recognised on returning after a gap of two decades.

There was one attendant who we nicknamed *four eyes*, because he wore glasses. He was the only attendant who wouldn't let children go upstairs, so if *four eyes* was on duty at the front desk we used wander round the Wildlife Gallery on the ground floor until his duty changed. We always went straight to the carnivores - lion and lioness, leopards, tiger and polar bear. To us they seemed enormous - have they shrunk in the intervening years? There was also a gigantic dried lobster, which I greeted as an old friend on opening a cupboard in the store room in 1991.

Going upstairs there were the mechanical models, and if you were lucky they would be switched on and moving, the fantastic glass walking sticks and a piece of rope, twisted twists of twisted strands. It didn't matter then that we were ignorant of the local glass and rope industries, we were just fascinated by the objects. On the same floor were the ship models, heaven to small boys brought up on *Airfix* kits. Who could forget the silver galleon, complete with silver cannons, which was really a salt and pepper holder?

What about the paintings? On the staircase was a giant painting of a spitfire (or so we thought), which looked like grey blobs unless you stood well away from it. This got us all doing 'modern art' in the painting class at school until the teacher put a stop to it. The Art Gallery had a sense of quiet and smelled of that same polish, had great colourful paintings and a roped-off chair which we thought must be very valuable. There was also a small room which only had small paintings - watercolours - in it, which you went through to get from the Art Gallery back to the engineering models.

Going upstairs again, up the 'staircase made of planks' we reached the greatest treasures. In the top corner by the window was the fossilised tree, then working backwards past some gigantic ammonites - how they have shrunk too! - and fossil fish, to the glass models of famous diamonds. We didn't quite take in the fact they were only models, but I can't remember stopping to wonder why the Star of India, Koh-i-noor and every other of the world's greatest diamonds came to be in our museum. Back round the corner to the boat carved out of a single log, a stone box containing a real human skeleton and with a baby's skeleton in there as well! We didn't care that these were local finds, but we took in the fact that they came from ancient times. We rounded off the visit with a quick look at the Roman and Egyptian Antiquities: I was fascinated by the needles and forks as much as anything else, then downstairs to

the cafe for a bottle of *Coca Cola* (with a straw, two if you were lucky) and a *Kit-Kat* bar.

That was our culture for the morning, and it was followed by lunch (always pie and chips) at the cafe in *Binns* then along to the cinema for, usually, a *Man From Uncle* film.

1972: First Impressions

By Neil Sinclair, now Senior Curator

When I arrived in Sunderland in 1972 to be interviewed for the post of Senior Assistant Curator (Branch Museums) I knew little of the town, apart from its reputation as a major shipbuilding centre, as the home of Pyrex, and as the centre for the production of pink lustre pottery in the 19th century.

My knowledge of Sunderland Museum was equally limited though I had already heard tales of Charlton Deas, as in 1922 his Deputy, Daniel Herdman, had become Librarian and Curator at Cheltenham, where I was a Museum Assistant.

I was extremely impressed by the well laid out galleries at Sunderland. The 1964 extension contrasted well with many other Museums in towns of a similar size, but was never reviewed in the pages of the *Museums Journal*.

Another good feature of the Museum that I noted in 1972 was its links with local societies and educational establishments such as Sunderland Polytechnic and Durham University. These were to form the basis for future developments, such as the creation of the Friends of Sunderland Museums at the end of the 1970s.

When I started work in January 1972 with the remit of developing Monkwearmouth Station Museum, I was also impressed with the friendliness of the staff. 25 years earlier, James Crawley had written to Jim Wilson that "staff relations are very cordial". One of the reasons for

Sunderland Museum's continuing success today is the good relations among the hardworking staff, with the exception of the inevitable staffing reorganisations which have been a feature of local government since the 1970s. It was perhaps fortunate in 1972 that I did not know that during the next three years I would be working for three different local authorities (Sunderland County Borough, and Borough, and Tyne & Wear County Council) and under four different Directors!

A reporter's perspective
Carol Roberton, of *The Sunderland Echo*

In the days when the Echo ran a page called *Wearside Echoes*, in which there were always gaps to be filled, I used to head for Sunderland Museum like a homing pigeon. I was even on friendly terms with Margaret Staff who ran the Tea Room in those days and who terrorised the attendants.

In those days, long before the county-wide museums service with its public relations department, dealing with the Press was an informal affair. It was best to time visits to coincide with the morning tea break when even Jim Wilson, the Principal Assistant Curator and later Director, would put down his hammer and preside over his staff at a huge oblong table - Jim wasn't much of a believer in sitting behind his desk with paper-work, preferring the practical tasks of getting exhibits ready for display. There was always plenty of news for Onlooker, the middle-aged male persona who was supposed to be the author of Wearside Echoes.

Often, strange characters would come in off the street, bringing with them all sorts of odd objects to be identified. And identify them Jim Wilson usually did. The most interesting pieces sometimes ended up in the collections, and these latest acquisitions were always worth a few paragraphs.

Then there were new members of the curatorial staff to interview, including Neil Sinclair, the present Senior Curator and successor to Jim Wilson as the font of all knowledge in Sunderland's social and industrial history.

There were grand plans for new galleries to report - and the great new venture of a museum in Monkwearmouth Station. I remember Marilyn Carr, then Asistant Curator and now living in France, dreaming up plans for the great platform scene to be called 'A Soldier's Farewell'.

The museum itself was a much quieter place in those days, of course. Footfalls echo in the memory of hushed galleries and the children's whispers. Videos telling stories, recordings of hammers clanging on steel to recreate the atmosphere of a shipyard, and cats that roared in exhibitions were all unheard-of.

The one thing that hasn't changed is the enduring popularity of the museum with Wearsiders, and although Onlooker is sadly no more, the Echo continues to feed readers' interest in their heritage. And despite the wonders of technology and the wonderful new displays, it was great to report a reader's nomination of good old Wallace the Lion for the first of the new *Exhibit of the Month* series this year. "I loved Wallace as a little girl and now my grandchildren love him too", said the letter - summing up just why the museum remains a family favourite.

Sunderland Museum Quilters
By Marjorie Elwen

Sunderland Museum Quilters began in 1985. After a few terms of learning the basics under the guidance of a teacher we decided to start a "self-help" group. Since then, we have made a number of patchwork quilts, cushions, bags and waistcoats. Members have group outings to Quilt Shows and Stitching and Knitting Shows around the country.

Our first Group Quilt was made to raise funds for the Body Scanner Appeal at Sunderland General Hospital. The quilt was raffled and raised £1,053. Charity work continues, and there is an ongoing programme of making cot quilts for a Romanian orphanage.

In 1988 we made "The Sunderland Quilt" using fabrics donated by FOSUMS: this featured landmarks in Sunderland and items from the Museum's collection.

Over the years we have taken part in "Activities Days" at the Museum, which we hope will generate interest in the craft among children, and encourage them to take it up.

In 1993 we made the Community Quilt, to be raffled to raise funds for developing the new gallery on shipbuilding in Sunderland. The project was so popular among children that we were able to complete two large cushions for children's prizes.

Our current project in 1996 is to make a quilt/wallhanging to celebrate the 150th anniversary of Sunderland Museum. It will interpret in stitch and fabric various items in the collection, and be a challenge for visitors to "spot the exhibit".

We find that a group of about twenty members is about the right working number for the group. Nine of the original ladies still remain, and there is a waiting list for new members to join.

In February 1993 the Sunderland Community Quilt project was begun to raise funds for the Shipbuilding Gallery. The Mayor of Sunderland, Councillor Bill Craddock (who was Chairman of the Tyne & Wear County Museums Service 1981-1986), the Mayoress Mrs Nancy Rowe, and Ken Douglas, "Mr SD14", Sunderland's best-known former shipbuilder, are seen here with members of the Museum Quilters and Fosums.

Councillor Ralph Baxter receives a cheque for £2,670 from Sybil Reeder, Chairman of FOSUMS, Marjorie Elwen, Chair of the Museum Quilters and Joyce Bishop, FOSUMS raffle organiser. The money was raised by special appeal, raffle and sponsorship of a quilt towards the development of the '... And ships were born' gallery.

FOSUMS - the Friends of Sunderland Museums

Fosums was launched in December 1979 with a special lecture by Dr David Bellamy, who subsequently became the President. The Friends have played a key role in widening the involvement of as many people as possible in the work of the museum since 1980. They have been extremely successful in the role of a support group when, like every other section of local government, the museum has been under financial pressure.

The achievements of Fosums have included raising funds for the museum, such as £3,000 for the new shipbuilding gallery. As a pressure group they helped to persuade the City Council to allocate all of the space freed by the library in 1995 to the museum, when there was a possibility that a large part might be used for the Registrar's department.

Fosums have also helped the museum in many other ways, such as with activities and publicity events. Their standard of catering at major openings has become particularly renowned.

The services to Fosums members include a monthly series of talks and a regular newsletter. Fosums membership for 1996 stands at 250, but they are always anxious to attract new members, and can be contacted through the museum.

TEN

SUNDERLAND'S BRANCH MUSEUMS

Monkwearmouth Station Museum

Monkwearmouth railway station was designed by Thomas Moore of Sunderland, and opened on June 19th 1848 as the Sunderland terminus for trains from Gateshead and Newcastle. George Hudson 'The Railway King' influenced the design of the building - he was chairman of the York, Newcastle and Berwick Railway Company and also M.P. for Sunderland. The station closed in 1967, and was bought by the Corporation in 1971 for conversion into a museum. Renovations included restoration of the original booking office which had remained little changed from 1866. The Museum was opened in May 1973 by HRH the Duke of Edinburgh

The adjacent siding area was acquired for housing rolling stock, and the footbridge and waiting shelter on the west platform have also been restored and added to the museum displays. One of the attractions of the Museum is that visitors can see trains on the Newcastle-Sunderland railway, which passes through the station.

In addition to the restored railway features, galleries were created in the museum's former waiting room and offices. The displays have been either about aspects of the history of the Monkwearmouth area, or about land transport. *The Stupendous Iron Bridge* (1996), commemorating the bicentenary of the Wearmouth Bridge, combines both themes.

A major development in 1994-95 was the outstanding success of the *Thomas the Tank Engine's Great Railway Show* which opened on July 16th and continued throughout the year. The exhibition resulted in the visitor numbers for 1994-95 almost trebling (60,183 as compared with

21,326 for 1993-94). The play area which was constructed for the exhibition at Monkwearmouth included a book-train and magnetic engine face board. These have obviously been major factors in attracting young children. The exhibition has also greatly increased the number of visits by school groups.

The Museum was filled to capacity during several of the days of special Thomas events, especially for the visit of Christopher Awdry who now writes the Thomas books. There were extensive Thomas-related events and activities ranging from Thomas Christmas parties to demonstrations of decorating Thomas cakes.

A baby-changing area was installed to coincide with the Thomas exhibition and has proved a valuable addition to the visitor facilities.

Grindon Museum

Grindon Close was the home of the Short family, well-known Sunderland shipbuilders. It was bought by Sunderland Corporation in 1953 and opened for use as a branch library, the first floor being converted for museum displays. At first, the museum space at Grindon was used for art gallery displays, with paintings and cases of art objects brought over from the central building. In 1970 it was decided to convert the displays as a series of 'period' rooms showing rooms and shops as they might have been in Edwardian times.

The remainder of the building was used for storage , mainly for the Social History and Ethnographic collections, because of lack of space at Sunderland Museum. When the former library area at Sunderland Museum became available it was decided to close

Monkwearmouth Station Museum. Left: The classical frontage of the Museum with children enjoying the Family Fun Day at the opening of the 'Thomas the Tank Engine' exhibition in July 1994. Right: The exterior of the booking office restored to its Edwardian condition.

Grindon Museum (in 1996) and transfer the collections and the budget for the museum to Sunderland.

Washington F Pit

Washington F Pit Museum is a former colliery winding house, housing the last vertical winding engine used in the Durham and Northumberland coalfields. After the colliery closed in 1968 the site was landscaped apart from the winding head gear and the engine house, which were restored by the Washington Development Corporation and it opened as a Museum in 1976 before passing to Tyne & Wear Museums in 1984.

The centrepiece of the Museum is the winding engine built by the Grange Iron Company of Durham, which is now powered by electric motor. The displays show the history of F Pit.

The National Museum of Music Hall

Sunderland's shortest lived Museum was the National Museum of Music Hall at the Empire Theatre, opened by 'Wee Georgie Wood' in 1974, independent of the other local authority museums. The Museum displayed posters, costumes and other exhibits showing the history of the Music Hall. The main feature was a replica music hall but unfortunately lack of an acceptable fire escape route prevented entry for the public, and this proved to be a major drawback.

In 1975 the Museum became part of Tyne & Wear Museums, but by 1978 it was decided to move the collections and staff to other museums and use the space for the newly-established Tyne & Wear Theatre Company.

The Curator of the Music Hall Museum was Joe Ging, who was an extremely well known theatrical personality in the North East. As well as his one-man shows and theatrical appearances, no North East television productions in the 1980s and early 1990s appeared to be complete without Joe Ging.

ELEVEN

OTHER MUSEUMS AND ART GALLERIES IN NORTH-EAST ENGLAND

Council-run, and other museums

Many of the councils in our area operate museums. For instance, Durham County Council currently runs the Bowes Museum in Barnard Castle, and Tynedale District Council runs the Border History Museum in Hexham.

There are also several museums, such as the Hancock Museum and Museum of Antiquities in Newcastle and the North East Aircraft Museum in Sunderland, that are not funded by local government, and they usually belong to societies or charitable trusts.

Following local government reorganisation in 1974, all of the council-run museums and art galleries of the five districts of Tyne and Wear - Sunderland, South Tyneside, North Tyneside, Gateshead and Newcastle - banded together to create a single body: the 'Tyne and Wear County Council Museums Service', now known as *Tyne and Wear Museums*. The five districts had very differing museum traditions. South Shields and Sunderland, had Victorian municipal museums that started off through the efforts of small local societies. Gateshead's museum came to the corporation as a single bequest from a wealthy benefactor. Newcastle Corporation had the Museum of Science and Engineering in Exhibition Park, and the Laing Art Gallery which was founded through a single large bequest. North Tyneside had no museums or art galleries.

South Shields Museum started in the mid

19th Century through the activities of several bodies: the *South Shields Working Men's Club and Institute*, the *Microscopical Society*, and *Geological Club* and the *Mechanics' Institute*. The two main organisations, the *Club & Institute* and *Mechanics' Institute* amalgamated in 1870,

and their building and museum in Ocean Road was taken over by the corporation in 1876. The museum at South Shields changed very little from the early 1900s until the 1980s, and it now has major new displays on the history of South Tyneside, and a programme of popular temporary exhibitions.

Gateshead at one time had the Saltwell Towers Museum in Saltwell Park. Built in 1871 for J.A.D. Shipley, a wealthy solicitor, Saltwell Towers was bequeathed to Gateshead Corporation in 1909. The collections were displayed at the Shipley Art Gallery until 1933, when Saltwell Towers was opened as a public museum. The building was suffering from dry rot, and closed in 1969. Gateshead, therefore, does not now have a traditional museum, although the Shipley Art Gallery includes a recent gallery on Gateshead's industries.

Considering its size and regional importance, it is perhaps surprising to realise that **Newcastle** has never until now had a general municipal museum. The Joicey Museum, opened in 1971, was developed as a museum of social history and Newcastle corporation's only major museum until then was the *Municipal Museum of Science and Industry* in Exhibition Park, built in 1929 as part of the Newcastle Exhibition and run for many years as a branch of the Parks Department.

If Newcastle was badly off for museums, **North Tyneside** was even worse. When the District was created in the local government reorganisation of the 1970s, it had no museums whatsoever. The Stephenson Railway Museum and Wallsend Heritage Centre were established in 1986, the last year of Tyne and Wear County Council.

The Museum Association and other bodies

Sunderland has played a prominent role in the history of a number of museum co-operative organisations. The Museum and Art Gallery, represented by J.M.E. Bowley and Robert Cameron, was one of eleven organisations at the founding meeting of the Museums Association at York in 1899. As a Member of Parliament, Cameron was able to raise questions on museum matters in The House on behalf of the Association.

J. A. Charlton Deas was closely involved with the Museums Association, and was its President in 1926-27. He was the first President to wear the Association's chain of office, which was commissioned from Richard Ray, Principal of the Sunderland School of Art and designer of the War Memorial in Mowbray Park.

The Museums Association continues today as the senior professional organisation that represents the interests of people working in museums.

In 1933 the Northern Federation of Museums (now called Museums North) was formed as a regional professional body. Charlton Deas was the first President and he has been succeeded by six Sunderland staff. Staff from Sunderland have also been very much involved in the several specialist 'panels' in Museums North, representing curators of Art, Social History, Natural History, etc.

The North of England Museums Service, (NEMS), part of a national network of Area Museums Councils, supports and promotes the work of museums in the region. Sunderland has been involved with NEMS since it was established in 1962, and both its councillors and museum staff have been members of its governing board. Councillor Ralph Baxter of Sunderland has been Vice-Chairman of NEMS since 1987 and the Chairman from 1996.

A significant development in museums in Britain since the 1970s has been the growth of nationwide specialist groups. Sunderland staff have again been closely involved with these and has provided officers for the Biology Curators Group, Geological Curators Group, Social History Curators Group, Group for Education in Museums, and the Museums and Art Galleries Disabilities Association.

Further Reading

G.E. Milburn and S.T. Miller's *Sunderland. River, Town and People* (1988) is an indispensable reference to anyone studying the history of Sunderland, and contains several references to the Museum and Library.

The *Library Circular*, published by Sunderland Library, Museum & Art Gallery at the turn of the century, includes a number of articles relevant to the history of the museum and sheds light on some of the characters involved in it. The Local Studies department of Sunderland City Library holds a set of this journal.

Over the years a number of reports have been prepared by committees and curators in association with the running and development of the Museum, and some have been published as small pamphlets. Sunderland Museum holds photocopies of these, as well as a photocopy of the catalogue of the Subscription Museum published in 1825, and of several reports prepared by committees and curators.

Back Cover: Section of The River Wear Map

The River Wear Map, completed in 1989, was organised by the education section in Sunderland. Twenty-one schools were involved in completing sections of the map, ranging from four-year olds in a reception class in an infants school through special schools to 15 year olds preparing for GCSEs. The map has subsequently been displayed on the wall of the entrance hall.